M E D
I C I
N A L
C H E F

The
MEDICINAL
CHEF
Healthy
Every Day

DALE PINNOCK

Photography by Martin Poole

Quadrille
PUBLISHING

KEY TO SYMBOLS

(S) Skin

(J) Joints & bones

(R) Respiratory system

(I) Immune system

(M) Metabolic system

(N) Mental health & nervous system

(H) Heart & circulation

(D) Digestive system

(U) Reproductive & urinary systems

THE JOY OF GOOD FOOD

I can't think of any greater pleasure in life than good food. It's one of the things I live for. I have enjoyed eating well ever since I was very young – I was the most experimental five-year-old imaginable when it came to all things culinary! I loved flavour, and lots of it. So for me, good, tasty, joyous food is an absolute must, and is something I'll never be able to sacrifice. But in my teens, because of my own health concerns (I suffered from bad acne), I started getting switched on to the science of nutrition and its role in supporting my health over the course of a lifetime. I soon realized that what I ate would make a world of difference. Many years of undergraduate and postgraduate study later, I'm now trying to show as many people as possible how food can be a very powerful – and literally life-changing – therapeutic tool. Food can be a medicine.

THE PHARMACY IN OUR FOOD

The food we eat affects us on every single level. Its components have a direct impact on the internal biochemical terrain of our body. They affect every cell, tissue and physiological function imaginable. With this in mind, it seems entirely appropriate to view food as a potential medicine. I see it as the one aspect of our healthcare that we can have direct control of; it's a great way in which we can actively engage with our own health. I am an absolute, straight-up and

outspoken advocate for the role of diet in healthcare.
I have no interest in being an alternative to anything,
and I don't see diet as any kind of alternative to
conventional medicine (although in issues like obesity
and early Type 2 diabetes, I can't see many more useful
interventions). I think food is a powerful and valid part
of the healthcare picture, something we can use safely
and enjoyably, no matter what type of treatment we are
receiving. Over the last few years I have formed valuable
professional relationships with dozens of general
practitioners, medical specialists and academics, and
my approach has wonderful support from people in all
aspects of healthcare. What I try and do is take the science
of nutrition and dietetics and place it in a practical
framework: the culinary arts. Rather than bombarding
you with science and technical data, I just show you what
to eat and why, no matter what your health concerns.

MY HEALTHY-EATING PHILOSOPHY

For some reason, which I have to admit leaves me
completely baffled, many people think that eating
healthily means drudgery, boredom, and leaving behind
everything you love in favour of rabbit food, smoothies
and endless tubs of houmous. If that was the case, I'd
have given it up years ago and would have been back
down the fast food joint faster than you can can say greasy
hamburger! But nothing could be further from the truth.
There's no reason why good, healthy, wholesome food

that will benefit your health shouldn't taste incredible. Healthy food can be decadent, indulgent and flavoursome, and give you pleasure at the same time as improving your health. So that's my approach to things – it's about real food in the real world. I create dishes that I look forward to eating. I think that's the key to staying healthy and keeping it that way: looking forward to your meals and enjoying every mouthful. I like to re-create my favourites, too. I love curries, pizza, kebabs – you name it, I like it. But I don't want to eat the unhealthy abominations you often find in the name of these types of dishes. With a bit of culinary creativity, you can have your favourite foods, and they can be good for you.

ABOUT THE BOOK

Healthy Every Day is not what it may seem at first glance. It isn't a collection of quick, simple one-pot wonders, although some of the recipes do tick that box. Rather, it offers solutions to the many scenarios in which people struggle to make healthy choices. Many people I've worked with over the years have had all the right intentions, and tried their hardest to eat well, but modern life being what it is, some situations – whether work or social – can throw a spanner in the works. This book is designed to give you ideas for tackling some of these hurdles. The recipes are practical suggestions rather than prescriptive absolutes; they're designed to give you inspiration for how to approach some of the problems that crop up. For some people, finding a good lunch at work is tricky. For others, breakfast on the go can prove challenging, with work demands and kids to attend to. You like throwing dinner parties but still want to keep it healthy? Well, there are solutions here too. It's just a way of bringing good food into the real world. It's not about complicated dietary regimes that would require you to have your own personal chef or the budget of Bill Gates. I'm going to show you how to make simple, affordable, amazing and very healthy food in a way you can easily incorporate into your life, no matter what your situation is.

This book really is all about the food. The science and technical data is there, but the real star of the show here is the recipes, which are organized according to the time of day and type of food you want to eat. If you loved *The Medicinal Chef*, here you'll find 80 brand-new, inspiring recipes that cover an even wider range of meals and situations – even grazing, cocktails and midnight feasts! The bodily system symbols at the top of each page mean you can easily see which conditions and systems each recipe can help with. The Star Ingredient sections focus on how the key ingredient will benefit your health, and Clever Combinations explain how one or more ingredients can come together in a dish to deliver an even more powerful boost. For further explanation about the nutrients in our food and how they work, refer to the Food Pharmacy section on page 164. All the recipes are good for many of the body's systems, but on page 176 you'll also find a quick-reference list of the recipes that help with each individual system, so you can focus on one area if you'd like to.

The recipe collection is even wider-ranging too, so there's really something for everyone here, no matter what your tastes are, from light Asian-inspired wraps and salads to home-comfort favourites and delicious puddings. The recipes are easy to adapt, and many of them are as useful to vegetarians and vegans as they are to carnivores. Nearly all of them are economical to make and use everyday supermarket ingredients. There's the occasional specialist ingredient that's worth seeking out, but these are not essential and you can easily swap things around. Just tailor them to your preferences or dietary needs, and away you go. Get in there, get creative, have fun and reap the rewards of better health!

Start the day

OK, we've all heard it a million times before, but breakfast really is the most important meal of the day. There's almost unequivocal evidence that eating a healthy breakfast will help control weight, sustain energy levels throughout the day, improve insulin sensitivity, stabilize mood... the list goes on. However, it's one of the meals that can prove to be a real Achilles heel for many people. Many of us have immense time pressures. Unusual working patterns, family commitments, school runs, early meetings, travel logistics – it can seem as though the obstacles are laid out one after another. With that in mind, we can feel forced to go for the quick, convenient options, which often means pre-packaged cereals or a quick slice of toast. Sadly, most of the commercially available breakfast 'foods' are sugar-laden, nutrient-devoid abominations, which come with rather clever marketing that would have us believe they're the most nutritious and healthy breakfast on Earth. In truth, most of them will do nothing positive for your health, and will assuredly cause havoc to your waistline.

So what are the options? Well, a healthy breakfast needn't be a long, laborious affair, nor need it be dry, chewy rabbit food – no call for hemp shirts here. It's easy to create a simple meal that will give your metabolism a kick in the eye, get your blood sugar levels up evenly, and have you leaving the house with a spring in your step, with a full stomach and sustained energy for the whole morning. You could have a simple egg breakfast, a smoothie made with coffee (yee-haa!), or for cereal-lovers, a delicious breakfast cereal made in bulk for just a few pence, or a refreshing smoothie. All the little gems here are quick, easy, satisfying – and very good for you.

Cheeky chilli chocamocha breakfast bomb

If you can say that one backwards I'll give you a fiver! This is a fabulous morning smoothie that will blow away the morning cobwebs with the subtlety of napalm. And you get your morning coffee. Get in! Coffee probably isn't the first thing you'd expect to see in this book, but its bad reputation is unjust. There are in fact many research papers supporting its health benefits – just leave out the sugar and cream.

SERVES 1

1 ripe banana
250ml oat milk (or use ordinary milk if you prefer)
1 heaped tablespoon raw cacao powder (or high-quality ordinary cocoa powder)
1 teaspoon honey or agave nectar (syrup)
1 shot espresso, or equivalent serving of instant espresso, cooled
¼ teaspoon cayenne pepper, or to taste
½ red chilli, chopped (optional)

Put all the ingredients in a jug blender and whizz up into a thick, luscious smoothie. Serve immediately, with ice and some chopped chilli on top, if you like.

STAR INGREDIENT: Cocoa is bursting with a group of compounds called flavonoids that have been shown to dilate blood vessels. They do this by stimulating the secretion of a substance called nitric oxide that relaxes the muscular walls of the vessels. Recent university studies showed that cocoa flavonoids can enhance cognitive function by improving blood flow to the brain. They may also provide a mild, temporary reduction in blood pressure.

Rose, cardamom & pistachio porridge

This is pure luxury, and a brilliant remedy for the breakfast boredom factor. It's just as quick to prepare as ordinary porridge, but has a flavour combination that will take you to heaven.

SERVES 1

4 cardamom pods
70g porridge oats
200ml coconut milk
1 teaspoon rosewater or
    4 drops edible rose
    essential oil
2 tablespoons crushed
    pistachio nuts
honey or agave nectar (syrup),
    to serve (optional)
crystallized rose petals,
    to decorate (optional)

Crush the cardamom pods with the back of a spoon and place in a saucepan along with the oats and coconut milk. Simmer for about 8 minutes, stirring, until the oats are nicely cooked. You can also add a little water at this point for a slightly thinner texture. Stir in the rosewater or essential oil, and mix well. Place in a serving bowl and top with the crushed pistachios, a drizzle of honey or agave nectar, if using, and crystallized rose petals, if you want to go the extra mile!

STAR INGREDIENT: Oats are awesome for naturally lowering cholesterol, as they're rich in a soluble fibre called beta glucan, which binds to cholesterol and carries it out of the body via the gut. Oats also provide sustained energy, and are packed with B vitamins.

Smoked salmon & leek protein pack

This feels really decadent, yet is very rich in nutrients. It's a simple, powerful breakfast that will keep you full for hours: eggs for protein and leeks as a great prebiotic to help boost the good bacteria.

SERVES 1
1 small leek
olive oil, for frying
3 eggs
1 large slice smoked salmon
sea salt and black pepper

Slice the leek into thin rounds. Heat a little olive oil in a large pan, add the leek and cook for 4–5 minutes, until softened.

Meanwhile, crack the eggs into a bowl and whisk them well. Season with salt and pepper. Add the eggs to the leeks and stir gently, keeping the mixture moving, to make a lovely leek-filled scramble.

Place the smoked salmon slice in the centre of your serving plate, and pile the leek scramble on the top of it.

STAR INGREDIENT: It's all about the oily fish here. Salmon is packed with omega-3 fatty acids, which are so often deficient in our modern diets. Research indicates that omega 3 helps improve cholesterol levels, reduce inflammation and improve mood.

Beetroot & smoked mackerel frittata

This may sound slightly bonkers, but it really is wonderful, and perfect if you want to try something new for brunch. I came up with it one morning when I had a few leftovers lurking in the fridge, and it has been a firm favourite ever since.

SERVES 1
1 ready-prepared cooked
   beetroot
1 smoked mackerel fillet
olive oil, for cooking
3 eggs
1 teaspoon sage (dried
   or chopped fresh)
sea salt and black pepper

Preheat the grill to high. Dice the beetroot and break the mackerel fillet into several pieces. Heat a little olive oil in a small ovenproof frying pan or omelette pan, add the beetroot and mackerel and cook for 2–3 minutes.

Whisk the eggs in a bowl and season with salt and pepper. Pour them into the pan, making sure all the ingredients are well spread out and are covered by the eggs. Sprinkle over the sage and cook over a medium heat for about 4 minutes, until the under side is cooked.

Transfer the pan to the grill and cook for about 4 minutes, until the eggs have set. Serve warm.

CLEVER COMBINATION: This is a real heart-healthy dynamo: beetroot has been shown to increase the production of nitric oxide in blood vessels, which relaxes blood vessel walls and can temporarily lower blood pressure, while mackerel is rich in omega-3, which improves good and bad cholesterol ratios.

Eggs royale
This is my favourite breakfast ever. There's a lot of butter in the sauce, but I have no issue with having a bit of what you fancy. It keeps you sane and makes you feel good; it's more a question of how often you have it, and what the rest of your diet and lifestyle are like. As a treat, this takes some beating!

SERVES 1
splash of vinegar
3 eggs
75g butter
juice of ¼ lemon
1 wholemeal English muffin
4 slices smoked salmon
sea salt and black pepper

STAR INGREDIENT:
Eggs are the perfect breakfast food, a very superior source of protein, minerals, choline, lutein and all manner of goodies. For a long time they were branded as dietary baddies, but we now know that they're true dietary heroes.

Bring a small saucepan of water to a simmer, reduce the heat so that the water is barely bubbling and add the vinegar. Crack two of the eggs, one at a time, into a cup, then slide them gently into the water. Poach for 4 minutes.

Make the hollandaise sauce. Melt the butter in a small pan. Put 1 egg yolk and the lemon juice in a small blender or food processor. Once the butter has melted, process the egg and lemon juice on a slow speed to break them up. Add the melted butter teaspoon by teaspoon, then, as the mixture begins to combine, slowly pour in the remaining butter. Once all the butter has been added, increase the speed and process until thickened. Season with salt and pepper.

Meanwhile, slice the muffin in half and toast both halves. Place 2 smoked salmon slices on each toasted muffin half. Top each one with a poached egg, then smother the lot in gorgeous hollandaise.

Mighty muesli OK, it's not all about muesli, but many people do like morning cereal, and provided you make your own and use good ingredients, they needn't be bad at all. The ingredients below are to make a bulk batch. Eat it with milk or yoghurt – whatever you fancy.

MAKES 1.1KG
500g porridge oats
150g raisins
150g goji berries
150g mixed seeds,
   such as pumpkin
   and sunflower seeds
150g chopped mixed nuts,
   such as walnuts and
   Brazil nuts

Mix all the ingredients together and store in an airtight container, where it will keep for about 2 months.

CLEVER COMBINATION: One of the pitfalls of many breakfast cereals is the fact that they're like sugar bombs, and can send blood sugar levels spiralling out of control. The combination of good-quality protein with complex carbohydrates will help stabilize blood sugar, and the oats, seeds and nuts provide exactly that.

Matcha mash-up
Matcha (powdered Japanese green tea) can be pricey, but it's becoming more popular in health food shops these days, and many people have asked me for interesting ways to use it. Plus, its health benefits are staggering and the flavour is divine. So here's one of my all-time favourite ways of using it, which brings back fond memories of summer in Japan.

SERVES 1

250ml oat or hemp milk
(or use ordinary milk)
1 ripe banana
3 teaspoons matcha powder
2 teaspoons runny honey
5 ice cubes

Place all the ingredients in a blender and blend into a thick smoothie. Serve immediately, with more ice if you like.

STAR INGREDIENT: It has to be the matcha really, doesn't it? Green tea contains some very powerful phytochemical compounds, the most widely studied of which is called epigallocatechin gallate, or EGCG for short. It has very high antioxidant activity, and regular consumption has shown benefits for high cholesterol and protection against atherosclerosis (thickening of the arteries). It also delivers some anti-inflammatory activity.

The breakfast monster Green drinks have become a bit of a healthy-living staple in recent years, and rightly so really. There's only one drawback: they often taste like the contents of a lawnmower bag. But I'm pretty sure this one will bring anyone round to the world of green smoothies. Try it... I dare you!

SERVES 1
1 handful curly kale
200ml apple juice
1 ripe banana
2 handfuls baby spinach

Pull the thick stems from the kale, leaving just the tender leaves.

Add them, along with the other ingredients, to a blender and process on the highest setting until smooth. Serve immediately, with ice if you like.

CLEVER COMBINATION: Let's face it, if you blend lots of green stuff together, no matter how good it is for you, it will still taste like drinking cabbage water! By adding the sweet fruits, their flavours take over and leave the grassy taste of the greens behind, so it tastes just like a fruit smoothie.

GOOD FOR: Eczema & skin health, eye health, high blood pressure, poor circulation, digestive health

The purple heart This is a super-easy smoothie that's bursting with flavour and is packed to the hilt with powerful nutrients. Great for getting you going in the morning.

SERVES 1
100g frozen blackberries
1 ripe banana
100ml purple grape juice

Add all the ingredients to a blender and blitz to make a thick smoothie. Serve immediately, with ice if you like.

STAR INGREDIENT: Blackberries are a great example of the power of purple fruits. The intense colour comes from a potent group of phytochemicals including the widely studied anthocyanins. These have been found to enter the cells of the blood vessels, where they can deliver effects locally, such as stimulating the release of nitric oxide, which causes relaxation of the blood vessel walls and lowers pressure within them.

GOOD FOR: Skin health, eye health, high cholesterol & high blood pressure, digestive health

The swamp donkey The weird name comes from the strange, sludgy colour of this drink. But don't let the colour put you off – this really is a powerhouse of a recipe, and tastes pretty good too.

SERVES 1

100ml apple juice
4 tablespoons frozen
    blackberries, plus extra
    to garnish (optional)
2 handfuls baby spinach
1 ripe banana

Place all the ingredients in a blender and blitz into a thick, if somewhat gruesome-coloured, smoothie. Serve immediately, with ice and a few more blackberries, if you like.

STAR INGREDIENT: Spinach is packed to the hilt with vitamin C and flavonoids, which deliver benefits for the cardiovascular system, the skin, eyes and even digestive health.

The perfect pear Smoothies don't have to be all about berries: pears are a classic English ingredient and have some fabulous health benefits too. This is ultra-refreshing and can fill you up for a good few hours.

SERVES 1
2 ripe pears
1 ripe banana
100ml apple juice

Cut the pears into quarters and place in a blender with the banana and apple juice. Blend into a thick smoothie. Serve immediately, with ice if you like.

STAR INGREDIENT: Pears may not seem very exciting, but they actually have some fabulous health benefits and are a potential part of the armoury in blood sugar management issues. They're rich sources of several compounds, including isorhamnetin and flavan-3-ols, that can help with insulin sensitivity. Plus, their high fibre content will slow down the release of energy from food, creating a drip-feed effect on blood sugar. The fibre can also help bind to cholesterol in the digestive tract and carry it away through the bowels before it is absorbed.

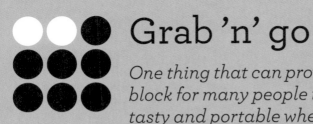

Grab 'n' go

One thing that can prove a bit of a dietary stumbling block for many people is having something on hand that's tasty and portable when they're on the hop. This doesn't necessarily mean breakfast or lunch on the go; what I have in mind here are snacks or munchies that just scratch an itch, and help you through those times when you might be tempted to grab a biscuit or packet of crisps.

Whether you're about to fly out the door to go and pick up the kids, or if you're rushing off to a meeting and want something to give you a quick boost between meals, these are ideal.

Nuts are an awesome little snack to have on hand: tasty, protein packed, filling and virtuous. Kale chips are a sure-fire winner, great for stopping you reaching for the crisps.

GOOD FOR:
Skin health, enhanced white blood cell function

Curry cashews

MAKES 200G
200g raw cashew nuts
1 teaspoon runny honey
½ teaspoon curry powder
sea salt

Preheat the oven to 170°C/325°F/Gas mark 3 and line a baking tray with baking parchment. Put the cashews in a bowl and drizzle over the honey. Toss them well until evenly coated.

Sprinkle over the curry powder and toss well again to make sure all the cashews are coated with curry powder. Season with sea salt.

Place on the prepared tray, spreading them out well, and bake for 10–12 minutes, until turning golden. Keep a close eye on them, as they can burn easily. Remove and let cool. Store in an airtight container.

STAR INGREDIENT: Many people worry about nuts being fatty, but they contain the good fats we need every day, so relax! Cashews are very rich in calcium and zinc, too: they are vital for supporting immune function and healthy skin.

GOOD FOR:
High blood pressure & high cholesterol, healthy gut flora & constipation, muscle function

Asian-spiced kale chips

MAKES 2 SERVINGS
200g raw curly kale
olive oil, for drizzling
1 clove garlic, finely chopped
1 small red chilli, finely chopped
1 teaspoon runny honey
2 teaspoons soy sauce
1 tablespoon natural crunchy peanut butter
¼ teaspoon Chinese five-spice powder
sea salt

Preheat the oven to 180°C/350°F/Gas mark 4. Remove the kale stalks and put the leaves in a bowl. Drizzle over a little olive oil and season with salt. Massage so that the leaves soften and wilt.

Mix the rest of the ingredients with 2 teaspoons water to make a rich sauce. Coat the kale leaves with the sauce.

Place on a baking tray and bake for 15–20 minutes, until crispy and crunchy. Remove and let cool, then store in an airtight container.

STAR INGREDIENT: Kale is bursting with magnesium, which is an important nutrient in reducing blood pressure, as it encourages the relaxation of blood vessel walls.

Cinnamon & black pepper apple crisps

This may sound a little unusual, but trust me, the flavour combination really works and makes a wonderfully satisfying snack that can be stored for ages and is perfect for staving off hunger pangs.

SERVES 2
2 apples
1 teaspoon cinnamon
black pepper

Preheat the oven to 110°C/230°F/Gas mark ¼ and line a baking tray with baking parchment.

Slice the top and bottom off the apples, then cut them into slices, removing the core section as you go. Put the apple slices in a bowl and sprinkle over the cinnamon and a pinch of black pepper bit by bit, tossing continually to ensure all slices are coated.

Place the slices on the prepared baking tray and bake for anywhere up to 2 hours, until crispy. Ovens do vary, so check regularly to see when the desired texture has been achieved. Remove and allow to cool on a wire rack, then store in an airtight container.

STAR INGREDIENT: Apples are great for anyone with high cholesterol because they contain a soluble fibre called pectin. This, like the beta glucan found in oats, can bind to cholesterol in the digestive tract and carry it away through the bowels.

Great balls of fire These tasty little bites give you masses of nutrients in one small mouthful: they're packed with B vitamins, essential fatty acids, minerals and all manner of other goodies. They also stimulate the senses.

MAKES ABOUT 16
200g pitted dates
50g goji berries
250g raw mixed nuts
2 teaspoons cocoa powder
¼ teaspoon chilli powder

Put all the ingredients in a food processor and process on the highest setting to produce a smooth, dough-like texture. Roll into small balls, about 2–3 cm in diameter, and refrigerate for 1–2 hours. Store in the fridge in an airtight container.

CLEVER COMBINATION: This is a great dish for enhancing circulation, thanks to the double whammy of cocoa and chilli. Cocoa contains a group of compounds called flavonoids, which get absorbed by the cells that make up the inner lining (endothelium) of the blood vessels. When these cells take in cocoa flavonoids they start secreting nitric oxide, which relaxes the vessel walls. This helps to enhance circulation and also to temporarily reduce blood pressure. Chilli contains a compound called capsaicin which has a similar effect, and also encourages the release of nitric oxide by endothelial cells.

Choc & nut oat bars
These are perfect when you're desperate for something sweet, rich and chocolaty – but they're as healthy as they possibly can be. Dark chocolate eaten in moderation can be very good for you. This doesn't pretend to be anything other than a treat. It's just a treat made good!

MAKES 6–8
130g unsalted butter
100g coconut oil
80g stevia (see page 145)
1 teaspoon vanilla extract
700g porridge oats
250g high-quality dark chocolate (70–80% cocoa solids)
120g natural crunchy peanut butter (with no added sugar or oil)

Melt the butter and coconut oil in a pan over a gentle heat. Add the stevia, vanilla extract and oats. Mix thoroughly. Press half the mixture firmly into a 23cm rectangular baking tin.

Break the chocolate into squares and place in a pan with the peanut butter over a very low heat. Melt it gently, stirring to combine. Pour this mixture over the first oat layer in the tray and spread it out evenly with a knife or spatula.

Top with the remaining oat mixture, press it down and chill in the fridge overnight before cutting into bars.

CLEVER COMBINATION: Oats contain a soluble fibre called beta glucan that forms a gel-like texture in the digestive tract, binds cholesterol and carries it out of the body through the bowels. Chocolate can have a temporary lowering effect on blood pressure, making this a great heart-healthy combination.

Date & tahini bites

Making a healthy snack doesn't have to be laborious. These are super-quick and easy and very nutritious, and trust me, once you try them you'll love them. It's the perfect option when your sweet tooth is nagging you.

SERVES 2
10 pitted dates
2 tablespoons tahini

Cut a small sliver off each end of the dates to flatten them, then cut them in half widthways.

Place a small dollop of tahini on each date half to make a sweet, creamy, bite-size snack.

STAR INGREDIENT: Tahini, or sesame seed paste, is very rich in several important minerals, especially calcium and zinc. It isn't always necessary to guzzle milk and dairy products to get enough calcium. Zinc is vital for many aspects of health, especially for a healthy immune system and healthy skin, not to mention helping the body to produce its own in-built 'house keeping' enzymes.

Sesame chocolate fudge This is a great snack that's perfect when you just want to reach into the fridge, grab something yummy and run. It really does have a chocolate fudge vibe going on.

MAKES 18
120g white sesame seeds
60g cocoa powder
3 tablespoons maple syrup
1 tablespoon coconut oil,
    plus extra for greasing

Toast the sesame seeds lightly in a pan until golden brown, then remove and leave to cool. Place them in a small food processor and process on full speed until they start to break down and a dough-like texture is beginning to form. This may take a few minutes, but stick with it. Add the rest of the ingredients and process until combined.

Grease a 20cm square baking tin lightly with coconut oil and add the sesame-cocoa mixture. Push down to fill the tin, making sure it is well compressed. Place in the fridge and chill for 5–6 hours, until firm. Cut into 2cm squares. Store in an airtight container in the fridge.

STAR INGREDIENT: Sesame seeds are packed with zinc, selenium, calcium and even iron. They also contain betasitosterol, which has been shown to deliver a cholesterol-lowering action.

Date & green tea oat bars

Green tea, or matcha, seems to be popping up everywhere these days. It's not cheap, but it's great for occasional use, and of course you can always leave it out. Its antioxidant properties make it an awesome mid-afternoon energy boost, or even a pre-workout snack. These bars are basically a raw flapjack.

MAKES 18

2 tablespoons coconut oil
2 tablespoons goji berries
120g pitted dates
1 heaped tablespoon matcha green tea powder
300g porridge oats

Melt the coconut oil gently in a pan over a low heat. Put the melted oil, goji berries and dates in a food processor and blend to a purée.

Stir the matcha and oats into the purée and mix well to combine.

Transfer to a 25cm square baking tin, pressing down well with the back of a spoon. Refrigerate until set. Once completely set, cut into bars.

STAR INGREDIENT: Green tea is a real powerhouse ingredient: it's well documented for having a very high level of antioxidant polyphenols, and it's even thought to help enhance fat burning in some situations by encouraging the body to use fats as energy rather than storing them. It's packed with magnesium, vitamins and a host of phytochemical goodies.

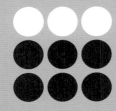

Lunchbox

In my line of work, people are always telling me that workday lunch times are often when their good intentions take a nosedive, thanks to the heady combination of ever-increasing work pressures, lack of time to buy or prepare anything decent and lack of options in the local area. Relying on vending machines or a mass exodus to a nearby pub or takeaway can soon create some very unhealthy eating patterns, and I remember how easy this trap is to fall into from my own office-bound days.

The good news is that it doesn't have to be this way. If you're serious about getting healthy and eating better, fantastic lunchtime fixes are only one step away. With a bit of organization you can make some dynamite dishes that taste good, give you variety, and most importantly give you a wide spectrum of nutrients. The key is planning ahead and making your own lunch. That way, you can control what goes into your food, and therefore into your body. It doesn't have to be complicated – taking just a little bit of time in the morning, or the night before, will really benefit your health.

Jumping jewelled quinoa salad

This is an awesome little salad that has loads of interesting tastes and textures. Many supermarkets now sell pomegranate seeds separately, and it's no longer the super-expensive fruit it used to be. You can easily double or triple the quantities to make enough to last you a few days.

SERVES 1

50g quinoa
2 tablespoons chopped
    mixed olives
½ orange or yellow
    pepper, diced
75g feta cheese, crumbled
1 tablespoon capers
2 tablespoons prepared
    pomegranate seeds
2 tablespoons olive oil
1 teaspoon balsamic vinegar
sea salt and black pepper

Place the quinoa in a pan and cover it with boiling water. Boil for 10–15 minutes, until just tender and translucent. Drain and leave to cool.

Assemble the salad by mixing the cooked quinoa with the olives, peppers, feta cheese, capers and pomegranate seeds and mix thoroughly. Whisk together the olive oil and vinegar to make the dressing. Add the dressing, season with salt and pepper and stir well again. Store in the fridge until time to eat.

STAR INGREDIENT: Quinoa is a fantastic starchy alternative to grains, and gives you that couscous-type fix without delivering too much sugar in one hit, which can have you reaching for those dreaded mid-afternoon energy boosters. It's very high in protein and releases its energy very slowly. It's also very rich in ALA, selenium, zinc and B vitamins.

Sensational salsa salad This dish is super-easy, super-tasty and really filling. No cooking involved, just a bit of chopping and mixing and hey presto, a nutritious lunch. So no excuses.

SERVES 1

4 ripe plum tomatoes
½ red pepper, seeded
    and diced
¼ red onion, finely sliced
small bunch fresh
    coriander, shredded
1 teaspoon cider vinegar
1 x 400g tin mixed
    beans, drained
sea salt and black pepper

Chop the tomatoes, retaining any juice. In a bowl, mix the tomatoes and their juice with the pepper, onion, coriander and vinegar, and season with salt and pepper to make a zingy salsa.

Combine the salsa with the mixed beans to make a satisfying and filling salad.

STAR INGREDIENT: Beans and pulses are a wonderful addition to your diet for several reasons: first, they assist in the removal of cholesterol from the gastrointestinal tract and add bulk to gut contents for better elimination. Second, they're a fantastic lean protein source. Third, they're rich in B vitamins and minerals.

Roasted root & rocket salad with honey mustard dressing This is great for taking to work on Monday morning if you've got leftover vegetables from your Sunday roast. The sweet roots with the peppery rocket are divine.

SERVES 1

1 small parsnip
1 carrot
½ sweet potato
1 tablespoon olive oil,
    plus extra for drizzling
2 teaspoons runny honey
1 large handful fresh rocket
1 heaped teaspoon
    wholegrain mustard
small handful nuts, such
    as walnuts or pecans
25g blue cheese, such
    as Stilton (optional)
sea salt and black pepper

STAR INGREDIENT:
Root vegetables' sweetness comes from oligosaccharides, which act as fuel for the good bacteria in our gut, stimulating their growth and replication. Bacteria regulate many aspects of digestion, from processing nutrients and breaking down food, to immunological function.

Preheat the oven to 200°C/400°F/Gas mark 6. Cut the parsnip, carrot and sweet potato lengthways into thin batons. Place them on a roasting tray, drizzle with olive oil, season with salt and pepper and roast for about 30 minutes, or until they are soft and beginning to brown at the edges.

Make a dressing by blending the honey, mustard and olive oil, and season with salt and pepper.

Remove the vegetables and allow them to cool. Mix them with the rocket leaves and toss with the dressing. Scatter over the nuts and crumble over the blue cheese, if using, and serve.

If you're taking it in a lunchbox, pack the vegetables, nuts and cheese at the bottom and add a layer of leaves on top. Take the dressing separately and mix together just before eating.

Supersonic soba noodle salad

I've been fortunate enough to spend a great deal of time in Japan, where I fell in love with cold soba noodles. They can now be found in any supermarket and are ready in a matter of minutes.

SERVES 1

100g dried soba noodles
1 clove garlic, finely chopped
1 teaspoon runny honey
2 teaspoons soy sauce
3 teaspoons sesame oil
1 tablespoon olive oil
6 cherry tomatoes, halved
¼ cucumber, sliced into strips
½ carrot, grated
¼ red onion, finely sliced
1 teaspoon sesame seeds,
   toasted
large sprig fresh coriander
   (optional)

Bring a pan of salted water to the boil, add the soba noodles and boil for 10 minutes, or until soft.

Make the dressing by blending together the garlic, honey, soy sauce, sesame oil and olive oil.

Drain the noodles well and and put them in a bowl along with the tomatoes, cucumber, carrot and onion, and stir well. Drizzle the dressing over the noodles and toss well to combine. Sprinkle with sesame seeds and coriander leaves, if using. This is one you can dress in advance and take in your lunchbox just as it is.

STAR INGREDIENT: Soba noodles are made from buckwheat, a great source of the phytochemical rutin. This can help strengthen blood vessel walls against damage, which can lead to atheroma (obstruction of the blood vessels).

The incredible isoflavone salad

This is great for those days when you need to throw some lunch together at a hundred miles an hour, but still want proper food. It has lots of flavour and texture.

SERVES 1

1 x 400g tin chickpeas, drained
1 handful fresh parsley, chopped
1 handful fresh dill, chopped
¼ cucumber, diced
7–8 cherry tomatoes, quartered
2 spring onions, chopped
4 tablespoons orange juice
1 tablespoon olive oil
1 teaspoon balsamic vinegar
sea salt and black pepper

Put the chickpeas in a bowl with the chopped herbs, cucumber, tomatoes and spring onions, and stir well.

Whisk together the orange juice, olive oil and balsamic vinegar to make a luscious dressing. Pour over the salad, season with salt and pepper and serve immediately, or pack in a lunchbox and store in the fridge until ready to eat.

STAR INGREDIENT: Chickpeas are a great source of isoflavones: compounds that are thought to have a beneficial effect on issues such as PMS and some menopausal symptoms, as they may be able to mask oestrogen deficiency problems, although the jury is still out on that. They also seem to help appetite control and cardiovascular health.

Bulgur-betaine box

Bulgur wheat is nutty and filling and goes well with many different flavours. I've used marinated tofu here, but you could add cooked chicken, fish or seafood, or mix it up to ring the changes. Bulgur is another ingredient that's great for stabilizing blood sugar.

SERVES 1

75g bulgur wheat
¼ cucumber, diced
¼ red onion, diced
8–10 raw sugar snap peas
1 handful baby spinach,
    finely shredded
½ red chilli, seeded
    and finely chopped
100g tinned aduki
    beans, drained
100g marinated tofu, cubed
1 tablespoon olive oil
2 teaspoons soy sauce
2 teaspoons toasted
    sesame oil
juice of ½ lime
sea salt and black pepper

Put the bulgur wheat in a pan and cover with boiling water. Bring to the boil, reduce the heat and simmer for 15–20 minutes, until soft and nutty. Drain and allow to cool.

Mix the cooled bulgur wheat with the cucumber, red onion, sugar snap peas, spinach, chilli and aduki beans. Season with salt and pepper and gently fold in the marinated tofu.

Make the dressing by combining the olive oil, soy sauce, sesame oil and lime juice and whisking well. Pour into the salad, stir well, then transfer to a lunchbox. Store in the fridge.

STAR INGREDIENT: Bulgur wheat is very rich in betaine, which supports liver function and the heart's ability to contract, and helps reduce inflammation and lower homocysteine, a marker of cardiovascular disease. Bulgur wheat is also very high in fibre, which improves digestive transit and helps stabilize blood sugar by slowing down the release of energy from meals.

Mackerel omega power salad with horseradish dressing This is a lovely fresh, zingy and flavoursome salad, and makes a really invigorating lunch – and a change from the usual sandwich!

SERVES 1

100g live probiotic yoghurt
2 teaspoons horseradish sauce
juice of ½ lemon
1 tablespoon olive oil
2 handfuls mixed salad leaves
6–7 cherry tomatoes, halved
½ red pepper, seeded
    and diced
½ small cucumber, diced
2 peppered mackerel fillets,
    skinned and flaked
sea salt and black pepper

In a small bowl, mix together the yoghurt, horseradish, lemon juice and olive oil to make a creamy dressing. Season with salt and pepper.

Combine the salad leaves, tomatoes, pepper, cucumber and mackerel in a bowl, dress with the horseradish dressing and serve immediately. If you're taking it to work, pack the dressing separately and pour it over just before eating.

STAR INGREDIENT: Mackerel has to be star of the show here, as it's packed with omega-3 fatty acids that are beneficial for the skin and nervous system. It has also been shown to improve good and bad cholesterol ratios, and to reduce inflammation in the cardiovascular system. The anti-inflammatory effect applies throughout the body, so for any inflammatory issues, up the omega 3.

GOOD FOR: Type 2 diabetes & weight management, high blood pressure & high cholesterol

Stabilizing salmon & quinoa tzatziki salad This is a gorgeous, fresh lunch. It's bursting with flavour, rich in nutrients, very filling, and its cooling, refreshing flavours revive your tastebuds. To save time, buy ready-cooked salmon fillets from the supermarket.

SERVES 1

50g quinoa
¼ cucumber, very finely
   chopped
1 small bunch fresh mint,
   leaves coarsely chopped
150g live probiotic yoghurt
1 bunch fresh parsley,
   finely chopped
1 cooked salmon fillet
sea salt and black pepper

Put the quinoa in a saucepan and cover with boiling water. Bring to the boil, reduce the heat and simmer for 10–15 minutes, until tender. Drain well.

Mix together the chopped cucumber, mint and yoghurt to make a creamy tzatziki. Season with salt and pepper.

Stir the parsley into the cooked quinoa. Season with salt and pepper and transfer to a lunchbox. Place the salmon fillet on top and smother with the tzatziki. Store in the fridge until eating.

CLEVER COMBINATION: This dish shows how meals should be composed in order to stabilize blood sugar. A lean protein source and source of good fats (salmon) with a low-GI complex carbohydrate (quinoa), together create a meal that releases its energy slowly, thus drip-feeding blood sugar levels, which greatly reduces insulin expression. Eating like this regularly can lead to greater insulin sensitivity, and more stable blood sugar.

B-vitamin booster wraps

This is perfect for munching at your desk, eating al fresco in the park, or wherever else you find yourself at lunchtime! It's tasty and filling and will keep your energy levels consistent throughout the day. You can buy pre-cooked salmon from the supermarket to save time.

SERVES 1

1 wholemeal tortilla wrap
1 tablespoon tahini
juice of ½ lemon
1 cooked salmon fillet
large handful mixed
    salad leaves
sea salt and black pepper

STAR INGREDIENT: Tahini is a super-rich source of thiamin, A.K.A. vitamin B1, which is essential for the health of the nervous system. It's great for bone health, since it has good levels of calcium and is rich in magnesium and copper, which are important for laying down bone. It also contains two lignan compounds called sesamin and sesamolin, which can help reduce cholesterol.

Lay the tortilla wrap out flat and spread the tahini over it. Squeeze the lemon juice over the tahini.

Flake the salmon into pieces and scatter them over the tahini. Season with salt and pepper, then put the mixed leaves on top. Roll up the tortilla and cut it in half. Eat immediately, or wrap in clingfilm and store in the fridge until needed.

This is best made and eaten the same day, but if you prefer you could mix the tahini and lemon and take it along with the salmon, tortilla and leaves separately, then wrap and assemble it at work.

Chicken & pink grapefruit powerhouse salad
This is a lovely dish that just shouts summer. It's great when you want something light and virtuous, or have a large evening meal planned. You could use a pre-cooked chicken breast to make it even simpler.

SERVES 1

1 large chicken breast
2 tablespoons olive oil,
    plus extra for drizzling
1 pink grapefruit
3 handfuls mixed
    watercress, rocket and
    baby spinach leaves
½ fennel bulb, very
    thinly sliced
1 teaspoon balsamic vinegar
¼ teaspoon dried mixed herbs
sea salt and black pepper

STAR INGREDIENT:
Pink grapefruits are packed with vitamin C, and their gorgeous pink colour comes from lycopene, which is thought to reduce cholesterol oxidation and benefits the health of the prostate gland. They're also rich in limonenes, which help protect cells from damage.

Preheat the oven to 200°C/400°F/Gas mark 6. Place the chicken breast on a baking tray, drizzle with a little olive oil, season with salt and pepper and cook for 25–30 minutes, until just cooked through. Allow to cool.

Meanwhile, peel and segment the grapefruit. To do this, cut the skin off with a sharp knife to reveal the flesh, moving the knife downwards and curving around the fruit to keep its shape. Cut into the fruit between the thin white membranes to release the segments, reserving any juices. Remove the skin, then slice the chicken breast and put it in a bowl with the salad leaves and sliced fennel.

Mix the olive oil, balsamic vinegar and herbs, whisking vigorously to emulsify. Season with salt and pepper. Place the grapefruit segments on top of the salad and drizzle over the dressing. Serve immediately. If you're packing a lunchbox, mix the chicken, fennel and grapefruit with the dressing and put it in the bottom of the box, then put the leaves on top. Store in the fridge and mix them together just before eating.

Cheeky chicken & lettuce roll-ups

This is a perfect for preparing the night before. It makes a great lunch as it has a very low GI, so it won't send your blood sugar levels soaring, thus avoiding the post-lunch crash. And it tastes a lot better than a petrol-station sarnie, that's for sure.

SERVES 1

3 teaspoons runny honey
1 teaspoon soy sauce
1 red chilli, finely chopped
½ teaspoon garlic powder
1 large or 2 small skinless
   chicken breasts
olive oil, for cooking
4–5 lettuce leaves
¼ red onion, finely sliced
handful salted peanuts
5–6 cherry tomatoes, quartered

CLEVER COMBINATION:
This one's more about what it *doesn't* contain; lettuce leaves replace starchy bread-based wraps or flatbreads, which can certainly cause blood sugar swings. It just focuses on protein and vegetables, which will keep you full and your blood sugar steady.

Mix the honey, soy sauce, chilli and garlic powder together in a bowl.

Dice the chicken breast into small pieces and add to the honey-soy sauce mixture. Stir well and allow to marinate for a few minutes.

Heat a non-stick frying pan over a medium-high heat and add a dash of olive oil. Add the chicken and any leftover marinade to the hot pan and cook for 5–6 minutes, until the chicken is cooked through and the marinade has started to caramelize and darken. Set aside and allow to cool.

Pack the lettuce leaves, sliced onion, peanuts, cherry tomatoes and chicken pieces in a lunchbox, keeping the lettuce away from the chicken so it doesn't wilt. Assemble the wraps by placing a few pieces of the cooked chicken, a few onion slices and a few peanuts into each lettuce leaf, then roll up and tuck in.

Silky celeriac soup

Celeriac is often overlooked and left on the shelf, but I love it. It has a fresh vibrant flavour and lovely smooth texture. Soups make a great portable lunch, too, because they're filling and easy to make in bulk.

SERVES 1–2

olive oil, for cooking
1 large white onion,
    finely chopped
2 cloves garlic, finely chopped
1 medium celeriac, peeled
    and diced, plus extra to
    garnish (optional)
750ml–1 litre vegetable stock
1 sprig fresh parsley, chopped
sea salt and black pepper

Heat a little olive oil in a large pan, add the onion and garlic and cook for 4–5 minutes, until softened. Add the diced celeriac and cook for another 5 minutes.

Add enough vegetable stock to cover, bring to the boil, reduce the heat and simmer until the celeriac has softened, about 10–15 minutes.

Transfer to a blender or use a stick blender to process into a smooth, silky soup. Season with salt and pepper and sprinkle with parsley. To make it extra-special, you could cut some thin strips of celeriac, fry them in hot olive oil until crispy and sprinkle over the top for a bit of crunch.

STAR INGREDIENT: Celeriac, believe it or not, seems to be a rather effective anti-inflammatory ingredient. It contains polysaccharides that deliver some localized anti-inflammatory activity to tissues it comes into contact with – those in the upper-to-mid gastrointestinal tract. It also contains a compound called 3-n-butylphthalide (3NB for short), which has a systemic anti-inflammatory activity.

Lycopene-boosting tomato & white bean soup This is the ultimate in quick fixes, and combines fresh ingredients with a few processed ones. It's fast, easy, delicious and still power-packed.

SERVES 1

olive oil, for cooking
1 large red onion,
    finely chopped
2 cloves garlic, finely chopped
1 x 400g tin chopped tomatoes
200ml vegetable stock
butter, for cooking
1 x 400g tin cannellini
    beans, drained
1 sprig fresh parsley,
    chopped (optional)
sea salt and black pepper

Heat a little olive oil in a pan, add the onion and garlic and cook over a low heat for 4–5 minutes, until softened. Add the tomatoes, bring to the boil, reduce the heat and simmer for 8 minutes.

Add the vegetable stock and a small knob of butter, transfer to a blender or use a stick blender to process it into a smooth soup. Season with salt and pepper.

Once smooth, return to the pan and add the cannellini beans. Heat through and sprinkle with parsley, if using, then serve hot.

STAR INGREDIENT: Although tinned tomatoes are processed, meaning the vitamin C may be lost, other powerful compounds actually become more absorbable as a result of the canning process. Tomatoes are very rich in a carotenoid called lycopene, and there is data showing a link between high tomato product consumption and reduced incidence of prostate enlargement. This doesn't demonstrate cause and effect, but carotenoids are good to consume regularly anyway, since they benefit cardiovascular health, eyesight and reduce inflammation.

Miso mushroom noodle soup My many escapades in Asia have given me a love of noodle soups. They're easy, filling and definitely a welcome change from the lunchtime norm. This recipe is designed to be made the night before.

SERVES 1

1 bundle dried soba noodles
   (they usually come in
   portion-sized bundles)
olive oil, for cooking
250g shiitake mushrooms
1½ tablespoons miso paste
small handful fresh
   coriander (optional)
1 head pak choi
sea salt and black pepper

STAR INGREDIENT:
Miso is a very nutrient-dense ingredient. It's rich in amino acids, which are essential for protein manufacture. It's also high in calcium, magnesium and folate and is a rich source of isoflavones, great for PMS and high cholesterol.

Bring a pan of water to the boil, add the noodles and simmer for about 10 minutes, until soft. Drain and toss in a little olive oil to stop them sticking.

Heat a little olive oil in a pan, add the mushrooms and cook for 4–5 minutes, until soft. Add the miso paste and stir well.

Top up with 400ml hot water and simmer for 1 minute, taste and season with salt and pepper if needed, then transfer to a lunchbox. Put the cooked noodles, coriander, if using, and raw pak choi in a separate container.

When you're ready to eat, break the pak choi into the miso soup, and heat the soup in a microwave or on the stove. Once hot, add the cooked noodles and coriander and serve immediately.

Magic mushroom soup Ha! That got your attention. Don't worry, this doesn't contain anything weird or illegal, it just has a divine flavour and texture that's rather magical.

SERVES 1

30g dried porcini mushrooms
olive oil, for cooking
1 large white onion,
    finely chopped
2 cloves garlic, finely chopped
250g chestnut mushrooms,
    chopped
250g shiitake mushrooms,
    chopped
3 teaspoons vegetable
    bouillon powder
sea salt and black pepper

Put the dried porcini in a heatproof bowl and cover with 400ml hot water.

Heat a little olive oil in a large pan, add the onion and garlic and cook for 4–5 minutes, until softened. Add the chopped chestnut and shiitake mushrooms and continue to cook for about 10 minutes.

Add the soaked porcini, the soaking water (leave any gritty bits behind) and the stock powder and simmer for 10 minutes more. Once all the mushrooms have softened, transfer to a blender or use a stick blender to process it into a smooth soup. Season with salt and pepper and serve hot.

STAR INGREDIENT: Shiitake mushrooms contain a unique type of sugar called a polysaccharide, which stimulates the production of white blood cells by interacting with areas in the gut known as GALT (gut-associated lymphoid tissue). These cause a reflex that basically puts the body in alarm mode and stimulates white cell production. The more white cells in circulation, the better the position we're in to fight infection.

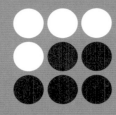

Grazing

Eating three meals a day doesn't work for everyone, and it's not always convenient. Some people find that eating a small amount every few hours helps keep their mood and blood sugar levels stable, and it can help with weight management too. Many people have also asked me for options when the nibbles attack, or for when they want to fill a hunger gap with something more substantial than a piece of fruit or some nuts.

Try some of these simple savoury fixes: the tasty dips are a great way to fill a gap and are made with everyday ingredients. I'm sure one of them will scratch an itch. They can either be made in advance and stored in the fridge, or whipped up in matter of minutes.

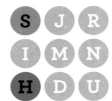

Cucumber canapés When you need a little snack that's bursting with virtue, these are super-easy and can be assembled in minutes.

SERVES 4
200g pitted kalamata olives
2 tablespoons olive oil
150g sun-dried tomatoes
50g feta cheese
½ cucumber
sea salt and black pepper

To make the first topping, put the olives and half the olive oil in a food processor and blitz slowly to make a coarse paste. Season with salt and pepper if needed.

To make the second topping, put the sun-dried tomatoes, feta cheese and remaining olive oil in the food processor and blitz at high speed to make a smooth, pâté-like texture. Season with salt and pepper if needed.

Slice the cucumber and top each slice alternately with the different toppings.

STAR INGREDIENT: Olives have many health benefits, especially for the cardiovascular system. They're very rich in a fatty acid called oleic acid, which is known to improve good cholesterol ratios and reduce blood pressure. They can also reduce histamine-mediated inflammatory episodes by interfering with the activity of histamine receptors and some inflammatory mediators. They deliver antioxidant benefits, too.

Heart-healthy red bean smoosh with crunchy crudités

This is very popular lunchtime fare at my house. We often end up chasing each other around the smoosh bowl with a carrot stick, trying to scrape up the last remnants. It's perfect for taking to work in a lunchbox, or as a starter or snack.

SERVES 1–2

1 x 400g tin aduki
   beans, drained
2 cloves garlic, crushed
juice of ½ lemon
4 tablespoons olive oil
a selection of fresh
   vegetables, such as
   carrots, celery, cucumber,
   peppers or radishes
sea salt and black pepper

Place the beans, garlic, lemon juice and olive oil in a blender or food processor, season with salt and pepper and blitz into a gorgeous, houmous-like purée.

Cut the vegetables into thin sticks or batons.

Pack the dip and crudités separately and chill until ready to eat. To serve as a starter, fill a bowl with the bean purée and place in the middle of a large serving plate. Surround with the crudités and devour.

STAR INGREDIENT: Garlic contains allicin, which helps to reduce bad (LDL) cholesterol. It also contains ajoene, which reduces clotting factors, making this an awesome dish for high cholesterol.

Baba ganoush with pitta strips

This dish makes a wonderful mezze, barbecue or picnic dip, or satisfying lunch. Many recipes call for the aubergines to be baked whole and the flesh then scooped out, but that's a mistake from a nutritional point of view, so I keep it on.

SERVES 1–2
1 large aubergine,
   cut into 2cm chunks
olive oil, for drizzling
1 tablespoon tahini
1 large clove garlic, crushed
juice of 1 lemon
2 wholemeal pitta breads
sea salt and black pepper

STAR INGREDIENT:
Aubergines are very rich in a powerful anthocyanin compound called nasunin. Some studies have shown that it can protect neurons from oxidation damage. There's certainly ample evidence that anthocyanins can benefit cardiovascular and cognitive health. So, in for a penny, I say!

Preheat the oven to 200°C/400°F/Gas mark 6. Put the aubergine chunks in a roasting tin, drizzle them with a little olive oil and season with salt and pepper. Roast in the oven for 20–30 minutes, until soft and beginning to caramelize slightly at the edges.

Remove and allow to cool slightly, then place in a food processor with the tahini, garlic and lemon juice. Season with salt and pepper. Process on full power until a creamy, houmous-like mixture has formed.

Toast the pitta breads and cut them into strips, then serve them with the baba ganoush. If you want to pack the pitta strips pre-toasted, tear them into strips and bake in the oven for 5–10 minutes.

Garlicky sunflower houmous

I'm a freak for houmous, and this version is nutty, sumptuous and very rich in a lot of vital nutrients. Great with veggie sticks, oatcakes, or if you're anything like me, just get the spoon in there!

SERVES 1
150g sunflower seeds
2 cloves garlic, finely chopped
1 tablespoon tahini
juice of 1 lemon
3 tablespoons olive oil
sea salt

The first stage needs a bit of time, so you need to start a day in advance. Put the sunflower seeds in a bowl, cover with water and leave for 24 hours to soften. Drain and move on to the next stage.

Place the sunflower seeds, garlic, tahini, lemon juice and olive oil in a food processor and blitz on the highest setting until a smooth, houmous-like dip has formed. Season with sea salt and store in a sealed container in the fridge.

STAR INGREDIENT: Sunflower seeds are worth a lot more than just rattling around in a bag of muesli. They're rich in a group of compounds called phytosterols, the very same ones that feature in well-known cholesterol-lowering drinks. They lower cholesterol by binding to it in the digestive tract and carrying out of the body. Sunflower seeds are also rich in zinc, selenium and calcium.

Kale, feta & dill pâté
This is a beautiful example of a dish that's easy to whip up and can be stored in the fridge ready for those moments when the munchies hit. It's great on an oatcake, with veggie sticks or even some multigrain toast.

SERVES 1–2

2 handfuls curly kale
100g low-fat soft cheese
100g feta cheese
½ teaspoon capers
5g fresh dill, roughly chopped
1 tablespoon olive oil
oatcakes or fresh vegetable
   sticks, to serve (optional)
sea salt and black pepper

Tear the kale leaves off the stalks. Bring a pan of water to the boil, put the kale in a steamer and steam for 5–8 minutes, until wilted and soft. Remove and run under cold running water, then drain and allow to cool.

Place the cooked kale and all the remaining ingredients in a food processor and blitz to make a smooth pâté. Season with salt and pepper and store in a sealed container in the fridge. Serve with vegetable sticks or oatcakes.

CLEVER COMBINATION: Kale is a fabulous fibre source and a very rich source of magnesium, one of the most commonly deficient nutrients, which is used in over 1,000 chemical reactions in the body. Pretty important! It also has antioxidant compounds called carotenoids, and the fats in the feta and soft cheese considerably increase our ability to absorb these.

Feed me fast

For me, the trickiest part of eating well is preparing something healthy after a long day at work. At the best of times my schedule is insane, and after a gruelling day the thought of spending hours in the kitchen trying to create a masterpiece would fill me with dread. Thankfully, good, healthy food isn't about culinary wizardry. And there's no need to rummage around for that dog-eared takeaway menu! Much of what I make at home these days is quick, snappy and takes very little effort. But it has to taste fantastic.

The weapons in your armoury here are the one-pot wonders, corner-cutting tricks and quick fixes, as well as ingredients that are easy to find. These dishes rely on simple preparation methods, the odd ready-made ingredient here and there, even batch cooking and freezing. In just a short time you can have something quick, delicious and healthy, and you'll know exactly what it is that you're eating. Get organized, get creative, and keep it healthy.

Pasta with peas, fennel, mint & parsley

Pasta, the ultimate quick-fix dinner, doesn't have to be a no-no if you choose wholemeal and have it with nutrient-packed ingredients. This gorgeous dish is flavoursome and functional, and the compounds that deliver much of the aromatic flavour are the keys to its beneficial effects.

SERVES 1

olive oil, for cooking
1 small fennel bulb,
    finely sliced
2 tablespoons frozen peas
75g wholemeal spaghetti
6–7 fresh mint leaves, chopped
1 sprig fresh parsley, chopped
2 tablepoons grated
    Parmesan cheese
sea salt and black pepper

Heat a little olive oil in a pan, add the sliced fennel and cook for 4–5 minutes, until softened. Add the peas and cook for another 1–2 minutes.

Bring a pan of salted water to the boil, add the pasta and cook for 8–9 minutes, or until al dente (check the instructions on the packet).

Drain well, add to the fennel and peas and stir thoroughly. Tear in the mint and parsley leaves and 1 tablespoon of the Parmesan, season with salt and pepper, and stir thoroughly again. Serve topped with the remaining Parmesan.

STAR INGREDIENT: Fennel is an unsung hero, but it contains several essential oils that ease bloating by relaxing the gut wall and dispersing gas. It also contains a potent essential oil called anethol, which has anti-inflammatory properties.

Red, white & green

This is the ultimate in easy, light dinners. It's the perfect solution to those days when you have literally dragged yourself home, and just need something quick, with very little to think about or do. If you like, you can even replace the houmous with the shop-bought kind for the quickest of meals.

SERVES 1

1 x 400g tin cannellini beans, drained
1 clove garlic, crushed
juice of ½ lemon
4 tablespoons olive oil
2 slices multi-seed bread
1 handful baby spinach leaves
2 plum tomatoes, finely chopped
sea salt and black pepper

Place the drained beans, garlic, lemon juice and olive oil in a blender or food processor, season with salt and pepper and blitz into houmous-like purée.

Toast the bread. Top with the baby spinach first, then the houmous, then the chopped tomatoes. Serve immediately.

CLEVER COMBINATION: Houmous is one of those dishes that's a great weapon in your arsenal for when you've pushed yourself too far or are feeling run down, and your immune system needs support. The garlic in it contains antiviral volatile oils, and beans are a great source of zinc, which is used by white blood cells to regulate their activity.

Bio-boosting okonomiyaki

A type of Japanese egg pancake, this is perfect for a fast supper. It's ideal for when you want something a bit naughty but still wholesome – a super-quick and tasty treat.

SERVES 1

100g wholemeal flour
2 eggs, lightly beaten
large handful kale, shredded
1 large carrot, grated
1 large leek, thinly sliced
2 tablespoons ground
   flaxseeds
1 teaspoon sesame oil
2 tablespoons soy sauce
1 tablespoon cider vinegar
1 teaspoon runny honey
2cm fresh root ginger,
   finely chopped
½ red chilli, finely chopped
coconut oil, for frying
sea salt and black pepper
salad leaves, to serve

CLEVER COMBINATION:
Using ingredients that are high in fibre and provide both pre- and probiotics, as leeks and kale do, helps digestive health from several angles, both short and long term.

Mix the flour, eggs, kale, carrot, leek and flaxseeds together in a large mixing bowl. You should have a bowl of batter-coated vegetables. Season with salt and pepper.

Make a dipping sauce by mixing the sesame oil, soy sauce, vinegar, honey, ginger and chilli in a small bowl, then set aside.

Heat a large non-stick frying pan and melt a small amount of coconut oil in it, ensuring the oil coats the base of the pan.

Place several large spoonfuls of the vegetable mixture into the pan, and press down to form a pancake. Cook for 2–3 minutes before carefully turning them over. Repeat until the pancake is crisp and golden. Slice into wedges and serve with salad leaves and the dipping sauce.

Potent pad thai

This is great for giving the immune system a kick in the whatsits, as it's full of some seriously powerful ingredients. I often make it with tamarind paste, but that's not always easy to come by, so it's fine to leave it out. Much better than a takeaway!

SERVES 2

125g flat rice noodles
olive oil, for cooking
1 red onion, halved and sliced
2 spring onions
2 cloves garlic, finely chopped
1 red chilli, finely chopped, seeds left in
75g shiitake mushrooms, sliced
juice of 1 lime
2 teaspoons tamarind paste (optional)
2 teaspoons fish sauce
2 teaspoons soy sauce
2 teaspoons runny honey
handful salted peanuts
small bunch fresh coriander, roughly chopped
sea salt

Put the rice noodles in a bowl and cover with hot water. Leave to soften – this usually takes around 15 minutes.

Meanwhile, heat a little olive oil in a wok or large pan, add the red onion, spring onions, garlic and chilli and stir-fry for 3–4 minutes, until soft and translucent. Season with salt. Add the shiitake mushrooms and continue cooking until they have softened.

Drain the noodles and add them to the pan. Stir well and reduce the heat. Add the lime juice, tamarind (if using), fish sauce, soy sauce and honey, and mix thoroughly. Tip on to a plate and garnish with the peanuts and coriander. Serve immediately.

CLEVER COMBINATION: This is an awesome dish if you are feeling a tad run down or feel the first signs of a cold. The combination of antiviral garlic, white blood-cell stimulating shiitake and decongestant chilli will give you a helping hand.

Bone-building five-spice squid

Don't be put off by squid: this dish has a heavenly exotic taste and vibe to it, plus it's so nutrient packed, it's almost too good to be true. It's one of those dishes that gets addictive.

SERVES 1

olive oil, for cooking
½ red onion, sliced
1 clove garlic,
    finely chopped
120g curly kale
dash soy sauce
2 large or 3 medium
    fresh squid tubes
½ teaspoon Chinese
    five-spice powder
1 tablespoon cashew nuts
sea salt and black pepper

Heat a little olive oil in a pan, add the onion and garlic and cook for 2–3 minutes. Pull the kale leaves off the stalks. Add the kale to the pan and continue to cook until it has turned a brighter, deeper green and started to soften. Add the soy sauce and set aside.

Heat a little olive oil in a griddle pan or frying pan over a high heat. Add the squid to the pan and cook for 3 minutes. Sprinkle it with the five-spice powder and season with salt and pepper. Turn over and repeat on the other side. Be careful not to overcook the squid; it should take no longer than 6–7 minutes in total.

Warm the greens, stir in the cashews, top with the griddled squid and serve immediately.

STAR INGREDIENT: Many people are cautious about squid, but it is a very rich source of selenium and zinc, which support the immune system. It's also a great protein source, and exceptionally lean.

Skin-boosting seafood one-pot

I have some good friends to thank for this one, as they made a dish like this at a dinner party once. I've played around with it a bit and it's become a household favourite. It's perfect on its own as a light dinner, or can be served with cooked quinoa and a side salad for something more substantial.

SERVES 2

olive oil, for cooking
1 large red onion, finely
    chopped
2 cloves garlic, finely chopped
500g tomato passata
1 skinless salmon fillet,
    diced into 2cm chunks
2 large or 4 small fresh squid
    tubes, cut into 1cm rings
150g raw shelled prawns
3 handfuls baby spinach
2 tablespoons chopped
    green olives
sea salt and black pepper

Heat a little olive oil in a pan, add the onion and garlic and cook for 4–5 minutes, or until the onion has softened. Add the passata and simmer for 3–4 minutes.

Add the salmon and simmer for 4–5 minutes, then add the squid and prawns and cook for a further 2–3 minutes, until all the seafood is cooked through. Add the spinach and olives, season with salt and pepper and cook for 2 more minutes, or until the spinach has wilted. Serve immediately.

STAR INGREDIENT: Prawns are an excellent source of the antioxidant mineral selenium. This is used by the body to manufacture an enzyme called glutathione peroxidase, which helps break down and remove waste materials.

Cold-busting wasabi salmon skewers

I love a good wasabi hit, and there's no denying the effect it can have on the respiratory system. The flavours of salmon and wasabi are a perfect match.

SERVES 1

2 skinless salmon fillets,
 cut into 3cm chunks
2 spring onions, cut
 into 3cm lengths
2 tablespoons soy sauce
1 teaspoon wasabi
 (paste or powder)
½ teaspoon runny honey

Thread the salmon chunks on to 2 or 3 metal skewers, alternating them with sticks of spring onion, and place the skewers on a baking tray.

Mix the soy sauce, wasabi and honey together to make a marinade and pour it over the skewers. Turn the skewers in the marinade several times to make sure all the salmon is evenly coated. Leave to marinate for 10 minutes, then turn the skewers again.

Heat a griddle pan or the grill to a high heat, add the skewers and cook for 15 minutes, turning frequently. Serve immediately with brown rice and a salad, if you like.

STAR INGREDIENT: Wasabi is a sure-fire winner if you're feeling in any way congested. It contains powerful volatile oils that work as an irritant to the mucous membranes in the respiratory tract, causing them to secrete a thin, watery mucous (ever had a runny nose at the sushi bar?). This helps clear any blockages caused by thicker mucous or catarrh.

GOOD FOR: Eczema & skin health; mood stability, depression & stress; high cholesterol; healthy gut flora

Tuna steak with herbed bean salad

Tuna steak takes virtually no time to cook – ideally it should be seared rather than very well done – and using cupboard staples like tinned beans means that in a matter of minutes, you'll have an awesome, nutrient-dense meal on the table.

SERVES 1

1 x 400 tin mixed beans, drained
small bunch fresh coriander
1 teaspoon capers
½ teaspoon white wine vinegar
olive oil, for cooking
1 tuna steak
1 lime, cut into wedges
1 red chilli, seeded and finely chopped
sea salt and black pepper

Rinse the beans under cold running water. Drain off as much water as possible and transfer them to a bowl. Tear in most of the coriander, add the capers and the vinegar, and season with salt and pepper. Stir well.

Drizzle about 1 teaspoon olive oil over each side of the tuna steak and season with salt and pepper. Heat a ridged grill pan until hot, add the tuna and cook for around 3 minutes on each side. Don't move it around; the edges should be cooked and the middle should remain pink.

To serve, place the bean salad in the centre of a plate and top with the tuna steak. Sprinkle with chilli and coriander and serve with lime wedges.

STAR INGREDIENT: Fresh tuna is preferable to tinned tuna as it retains its omega-3 fatty acids, which are vital for heart, skin and brain health, and for regulating inflammation (the oils in tinned tuna are removed and sold to the dietary supplements industry). Tuna is also very rich in selenium, which is used to make enzymes that remove waste products from our cells.

Mozzarella chicken protein pack

This is at the slightly naughtier end of the spectrum, but it's very filling and a great protein hit to boot. I often make it as a light dinner with a side salad on days when I have done any resistance workouts, or really pushed myself and need to up my protein.

SERVES 1

1 large chicken breast
olive oil, for drizzling
3 handfuls baby spinach leaves
1 tablespoon olive tapenade
    (optional)
2 slices low-fat mozzarella
sea salt and black pepper

CLEVER COMBINATION:
Spinach is a very rich source of the antioxidant beta carotene, a fat-soluble nutrient, and the mozzarella obviously has a natural fat content. This works as a carrier for the beta carotene, which is a great anti-inflammatory, and significantly increases your absorption of it.

Preheat the oven to 190°C/375°F/Gas mark 5. Place the chicken breast on a baking tray, drizzle with a little olive oil, season with salt and pepper and roast for 20 minutes.

Meanwhile, place the spinach leaves in a metal sieve or colander and slowly pour boiling water over them until wilted. Squeeze all of the water out and leave to drain.

After 20 minutes, remove the tray from the oven. Carefully spread a layer of tapenade, if using, on top of the chicken breast, cover with the wilted spinach, then place the mozzarella on top of the spinach. Season with salt and pepper. Return to the oven for another 8 minutes, until golden and bubbling. Remove and leave to rest for a few minutes before eating.

Can-do chicken kebab

This is a quick and healthy version of the takeaway favourite. No grease, just clean, fresh ingredients. When you see the takeaway, keep on driving and make this bad boy when you get home instead.

SERVES 1

1 large skinless chicken breast
olive oil, for cooking
juice of ½ lemon
1 wholemeal pitta bread
2 teaspoons mayonnaise
1 handful mixed salad leaves
3–4 cherry tomatoes, quartered
sea salt and black pepper

CLEVER COMBINATION:
This is great for stabilizing blood sugar, whether due to stress, weight management or more serious issues such as Type 2 diabetes. The combination of high-quality complex carbohydrates and lean proteins create a meal that releases its energy slowly, thus drip-feeding blood sugar and keeping levels stable.

Preheat the oven to 200°C/400°F/Gas mark 6. Heat a ridged grill pan until hot, drizzle the chicken with olive oil and season with salt and pepper. Add the chicken to the pan and cook, without moving it, for 3–4 minutes, until you have griddle marks. Turn it over, transfer to a baking tray, squeeze the lemon juice over it and roast for around 15 minutes, until cooked through. (Alternatively, simply roast the chicken in the oven for 20 minutes). Set aside to rest for a few minutes.

Warm the pitta bread and cut it in half to make 2 pockets. Slice the chicken. Line each pitta pocket with a little mayonnaise, add some salad leaves and tomatoes and half the chicken. Repeat with the other pitta pocket and serve immediately.

Lazy weekends

To me, there is no greater joy in life than sharing good food, good wine and good times with friends and family. And there's absolutely no reason why this – which is true nutrition for the soul – shouldn't be just as healthy as any other part of your diet. Many of us who love to entertain sometimes feel we have to throw our dietary efforts out of the window the minute a dinner party is planned; for some reason, we've disconnected healthy foods from decadence, as though food has to be one or the other. But that's no way to live. There's no reason why you can't create special feasts and actively support your health at the same time. You can go the extra mile, make beautiful dinner-party spreads and still keep your commitment to good food and healthier living – and here are plenty of suggestions to show you how. All the recipes are easy to double or triple to feed more people.

Also in this section are some dishes that are great for when you have a little more time on your hands and can get a bit fancier. These aren't necessarily dinner-party goodies, just dishes for those days when you can spend a bit more time in the kitchen getting creative.

One-pot Moroccan vegetable tagine

I do love a good tagine. This is a really
easy dish, but it tastes superb after
its slow simmering.

SERVES 4
olive oil, for cooking
2 large red onions,
   finely chopped
4 cloves garlic,
   finely chopped
800g tomato passata
16 pitted dates, chopped
2 teaspoons ground
   cinnamon, or 2
   cinnamon sticks
1 teaspoon ground cumin
2 x 400g tins chickpeas,
   drained
2 large red peppers,
   cut into 2cm chunks
1 large aubergine,
   cut into 1cm chunks
2 large courgettes, cut
   into half-moon slices
sea salt and black pepper
fresh coriander sprigs,
   to serve

Heat a little olive oil in a pan, add the onions
and garlic and cook for 4–5 minutes, until
softened. Add the passata, dates, cinnamon
and cumin and simmer for 10–15 minutes,
stirring frequently.

Add the chickpeas, peppers and aubergine
and simmer for 20 minutes, stirring frequently.
If the sauce gets too dry, add a little water, but
bear in mind the sauce should be quite thick
at the end. Add the courgettes and simmer
for a further 10 minutes. Season with salt and
pepper. Serve hot, sprinkled with coriander,
along with wholemeal couscous or quinoa.

STAR INGREDIENT: Cinnamon has been used for
decades by herbalists to encourage blood flow and
as a mild circulatory stimulant. Some studies have
shown that cinnamon extracts may be useful for
stabilizing blood sugar levels and making cells more
responsive to insulin signalling, although they have
yet to be tested on humans. Still, it's interesting stuff.

Beet balsamic bake with sweet potato topping

This is perfect comfort food for me, a really warming treat. Sweet potato and beetroot make a perfect marriage, and the sharpness of the balsamic vinegar gives a wonderful balance.

SERVES 4

8 large raw beetroot, scrubbed and cut into wedges
4 tablespoons olive oil
2 tablespoons balsamic vinegar
6 large sweet potatoes, peeled and cut into large dice
1½ tablespoons wholegrain mustard
½ teaspoon cornflour
sea salt and black pepper
baby salad leaves, to serve (optional)

STAR INGREDIENT:
Beetroot has become a lot more popular these days, and I'm glad it has! It's wonderful for heart health thanks to its nitrate content. This helps the body to produce nitric oxide, which widens blood vessels and lowers the pressure inside them.

Preheat the oven to 200°C/400°F/Gas mark 6. Place the beetroot wedges on a baking sheet, drizzle with olive oil and 1 tablespoon balsamic vinegar and roast for 20–30 minutes, until soft and beginning to caramelize around the edges.

Meanwhile, place the diced sweet potatoes in a pan, cover with boiling water and simmer for 10–15 minutes, or until soft. Drain and return them to the pan. Add the mustard, season with salt and pepper, and mash to the finest texture you can.

Place the roasted beetroot in a baking dish, then add 2–3 tablespoons water to the pan that the beetroot was roasted in, and stir well to dislodge flavours and any bits of caramelized beetroot left behind from the roasting. Add the cornflour and stir well until thickened. Pour the liquid over the beetroot in the baking dish.

Top the beetroot with the sweet potato mash and bake in the oven for 15 minutes, or until lightly golden and crunchy. Serve with a baby leaf salad on the side, if you like.

Immuno-falafels with quinoa & tahini

These are a healthier version of the usual deep-fried falafel. The problem with deep-frying is that oils kept at high temperatures for a long time will develop what are known as trans fats, which are toxic and much worse for you than any fat on its own could be.

SERVES 4

200g quinoa
4 teaspoons bouillon powder
1 teaspoon cinnamon
2 tablespoons raisins
2 tablespoons sliced almonds
25g fresh parsley, chopped
2 x 400g tins chickpeas
4 cloves garlic, crushed
2 teaspoons ground cumin
1 teaspoon ground coriander
1 red onion, finely chopped
2 eggs, lightly beaten
2 tablespoons wholemeal flour
1 tablespoon olive oil,
    plus extra for frying
1½ tablespoons tahini
juice of ½ lemon
sea salt and black pepper

CLEVER COMBINATION:
The double whammy of antiviral garlic and zinc-packed chickpeas makes this great for immune health.

Put the quinoa in a pan, cover with boiling water, add the bouillon powder and simmer for 20 minutes, until soft. Drain and stir in the cinnamon, raisins, almonds and half the parsley.

Place the chickpeas, half the garlic, the remaining parsley, cumin and coriander in a food processor and blitz to a paste. Transfer to a bowl, add the onion, eggs and flour, season with salt and pepper and mix well to form a stiff mixture.

Preheat the oven to 200°C/400°F/Gas mark 6 and line a baking tray with baking parchment. Shape into small patties and fry in a little olive oil for 2–3 minutes on each side, until starting to turn crispy. Transfer to the baking sheet and bake for 10–12 minutes.

Meanwhile, make the dressing by whisking together the tahini, olive oil, remaining garlic and lemon juice, and seasoning with salt and pepper. Serve the falafels with the quinoa and tahini dressing.

Antioxidant penne with pepper paprika sauce This lovely dish is full of flavour, simple to make, and packed with a wide range of potent compounds and nutrients.

SERVES 4

4 large red peppers, diced
2 small red onions,
    coarsely chopped
2 cloves garlic,
    finely chopped
200g cherry tomatoes,
    halved
olive oil, for drizzling
1 tablespoon sweet
    smoked paprika
300g wholemeal penne
100g feta cheese,
    crumbled (optional)
sea salt and black pepper

Preheat the oven to 200°C/400°F/Gas mark 6. Put the peppers, onions, garlic and tomatoes in a roasting tin, drizzle with olive oil, season with salt and pepper and mix well. Sprinkle over the smoked paprika, stir well and roast for 20–25 minutes, stirring several times, until the edges of the vegetables have caramelized slightly.

Bring a large pan of salted water to the boil, add the pasta and cook for 7–8 minutes, until al dente (check the instructions on the packet).

Place the roasted vegetables in a blender or food processor and process into a smooth, luscious sauce. Drain the pasta, toss in the sauce and serve immediately, sprinkled with crumbled feta, if you like.

STAR INGREDIENT: Red peppers are packed with a host of nutrients and active compounds, and one of the most powerful are the flavonoids responsible for the deep red colour. These have anti-inflammatory and antioxidant activity. So, when choosing your peppers, the darker the colour, the more antioxidants there are!

Aubergine & green lentil comfort bake

This is super-filling and wholesome, but has no nasties. It's great for days when you're starving, or for cold, drizzly days when you need something warming and nurturing.

SERVES 4

olive oil, for cooking
2 large red onions,
    finely chopped
4 cloves garlic, finely chopped
2 x 400g tins cooked green
    lentils, drained
750g tomato passata
1½ teaspoons dried
    mixed herbs
2 aubergines, sliced
low-fat mozzarella, torn
    into pieces, to serve
sea salt and black pepper

STAR INGREDIENT:
Lentils are great for both short and long-term digestive health. In the short term, they're a great fibre source, and help to keep things moving. In the long term they can boost the natural bacterial colony that lives in the digestive system by providing certain sugars as a food source, causing them to reproduce and flourish.

Heat a little olive oil in a large pan, add the onions and garlic and cook for 4–5 minutes, until softened. Add the lentils, passata and mixed herbs and simmer gently for 15 minutes, until you have a thick, luscious tomato sauce. Season with salt and pepper.

Heat a little more olive oil in a frying pan, add the aubergine slices and fry for 3–4 minutes, turning frequently, until slightly translucent. Season with salt and pepper.

Preheat the oven to 200°C/400°F/Gas mark 6. Begin layering the bake by placing a few slices of aubergine at the bottom of a baking dish. Top with a layer of tomato and lentil sauce, then continue adding alternating layers until all the ingredients are used up. Sprinkle the mozzarella on top and bake for 10 minutes, until bubbling and melted. Serve hot.

Chickpeas, spinach & cashews with cumin & coconut
This is quite a simple dish, but its unusual flavours make it great for entertaining, especially if you have vegetarian guests. It can make a wonderful main dish or even an exciting side.

SERVES 4

olive oil, for cooking
2 large onions,
    finely chopped
4 cloves garlic,
    finely chopped
600g baby spinach leaves
2 x 400g tins chickpeas,
    drained
300g raw cashew nuts
100g goji berries
1 teaspoon ground cumin
2 tablespoons desiccated
    coconut
sea salt and black pepper

Heat a little olive oil in a pan, add the onions and garlic and cook for 4–5 minutes, until softened. Stir in the baby spinach and cook until it wilts.

Add the chickpeas, cashew nuts, goji berries and cumin, and cook for another 3 minutes. Season with salt and pepper. Heat another pan, add the coconut and toast for 1–2 minutes, until lightly golden. Sprinkle the toasted coconut over the chickpeas and serve hot. It's great with a salad or sautéed green vegetables.

STAR INGREDIENT: Cumin has been used in herbal medicine for centuries as a carminative, which means it can ease gas, bloating and digestive discomfort. It also contains several anti-inflammatory and analgesic compounds, which may help relieve residual inflammation in the digestive tract.

Blooming bean burgers with red cabbage & apple slaw

Bean burgers are still often seen as fit only for vegetarian barbecues, but a good one can be really tasty. With its spices and a lovely slaw, this one is quite special.

SERVES 4

2 x 400g tins mixed
   beans, drained
150g wholemeal breadcrumbs
3 teaspoons Madras
   curry paste
2 eggs, lightly beaten
large bunch fresh coriander,
   roughly chopped
2 large apples, cored
   and grated
1 small red cabbage, shredded
300g live probiotic yoghurt
2 teaspoons mustard seeds
4 wholemeal burger buns,
   toasted (optional)
sea salt and black pepper

Put the beans in a bowl and mash them coarsely with a potato masher or a firm fork. Add the breadcrumbs, curry paste, eggs and coriander, season with salt and pepper and stir well.

Preheat the grill to high and line a baking tray with kitchen foil. Shape the bean mixture into 4 burger patties, place them on the baking tray and under the hot grill. Grill for 10–15 minutes, turning frequently, until crisp and golden.

Meanwhile, make the slaw by mixing the apple and cabbage with the yoghurt and mustard seeds, and season with salt and pepper. Serve the burgers with the slaw, and toasted wholemeal burger buns, if you like.

STAR INGREDIENT: Red cabbage is packed with anthocyanins, which are responsible for its purple colour, and have been shown to strengthen and encourage relaxation of blood vessel walls, reducing blood pressure. It's also rich in glucosinolates, and although I'm ultra-cautious about the risks or benefits of specific foods for cancer, there is evidence that glucosinolates can offer some protection against some forms of cancers.

White bean & winter squash stew

This is a gorgeous, hearty winter warmer, and low GI and low calorie to boot. I usually just have a bowlful of this as it is, or sometimes with a side salad.

SERVES 4

olive oil, for cooking
2 large red onions, finely chopped
2 cloves garlic, finely chopped
2 tablespoons miso paste
2 x 400g tins butter beans, drained
2 x 400g tins cannellini beans, drained
1 large winter squash, such as butternut, seeded and coarsely diced, skin on
1 litre light vegetable stock
sea salt and black pepper

Heat a little olive oil in a small pan, add the onions and garlic and cook for 4–5 minutes, until softened. Stir in the miso paste, beans and chopped squash. Add a little of the vegetable stock and bring to a simmer. As the stock reduces, keep it topped up.

Keep simmering until the squash is nice and soft – about 30 minutes. There should be just enough liquid to create a thick stew. Adding the stock bit by bit will mean that the starch from the beans creates this texture. If you add too much stock it will be too watery. Season with salt and pepper and serve hot.

STAR INGREDIENT: Squash can be a real powerhouse of nutrition, especially the yellow- and orange-fleshed varieties. These are rich in carotenoids such as beta carotene, which offer antioxidant and anti-inflammatory activity, especially for the skin. They're also rich in B vitamins and fibre.

GOOD FOR: High cholesterol, constipation & healthy gut flora

Spring-in-your-step barley risotto

I'm a real fan of risottos, and I love substituting pearl barley for the usual Arborio rice. Not only does it give you a new texture, but it also ups the nutritional profile of the dish. It takes slightly longer to cook than a regular risotto, but it's so worth the wait.

SERVES 4

olive oil, for cooking
2 onions, finely chopped
4 cloves garlic, finely chopped
500g chestnut mushrooms, sliced
500g pearl barley
750ml–1.5 litres vegetable stock
6 large leaves Swiss chard, shredded
8 spring onions, sliced
2 tablespoons grated Parmesan cheese
sea salt and black pepper

Heat a little olive oil in a large pan, add the onions and garlic and cook for 4–5 minutes, until softened. Add the mushrooms and cook for a further 5 minutes.

Add the pearl barley and 200ml vegetable stock. Cook, stirring, until the liquid is nearly absorbed, and continue adding stock every few minutes, as if you were making a normal risotto.

Continue cooking until the barley has softened and the dish begins to take on a creamy texture. At this stage, season with salt and pepper, add the chard and continue cooking until it wilts. Finally, stir in the spring onions, Parmesan and a little more stock, and serve immediately.

STAR INGREDIENT: Pearl barley is quite an important addition to the cholesterol-lowering arsenal. It contains a compound called propionic acid, which has been shown in animal studies to reduce an enzyme called HMG-CoA reductase, which is involved in synthesizing cholesterol. Its high fibre content also helps carry cholesterol out of the body via the bowel.

No-stress pesto cod with greeny beany mash This tastes awesome: fresh, clean and nutrient packed. It gives you easily digestible protein, fibre, bucketfuls of minerals... oh, and it looks pretty impressive too.

SERVES 4

4 skinless cod fillets
2 x 400g tins broad
    beans, drained
olive oil, for cooking
1 onion, finely chopped
6 tablespoons breadcrumbs
    (shop-bought or
    home-made)
2 tablespoons green pesto
large bunch fresh parsley,
    coarsely chopped
2 tablespoons chopped
    green olives
sea salt and black pepper

STAR INGREDIENT:
Parsley contains a unique
group of essential oils that
actually stimulate kidney
output, increasing urine
volume. It was used by
herbalists to reduce
water retention.

Preheat the oven to 200°C/400°F/Gas mark 6 and line a baking tray with foil. Place the cod fillets on the tray and bake for 8–10 minutes, until almost cooked through.

Meanwhile, place the broad beans in a small pan and top with boiling water. Simmer for 5 minutes to warm through and soften slightly, then drain. Heat a little olive oil in a separate pan, add the onion and cook gently for 4–5 minutes, until softened.

Mix the breadcrumbs and pesto together. Remove the cod from the oven and top with the pesto crumbs. Return to the oven for another 5–6 minutes.

Return the drained broad beans to the pan along with the cooked onion and parsley, then mash to form a coarse mash. Stir in the chopped olives and season with salt and pepper. To serve, place a dollop of the mash in the centre of a plate and top with the cod fillet.

Heart-healthy Sicilian cod with spinach
This is a lovely light dish that oozes sunny flavours – perfect for summer entertaining. Fresh, vibrant, clean: good food at its best.

SERVES 4

olive oil, for cooking
   and drizzling
3 red onions, finely chopped
4 cloves garlic, finely chopped
2 x 400g tins chopped
   tomatoes
6 tablespoons chopped
   black olives
6 sprigs fresh oregano, torn
4 medium cod fillets
juice of 1 lemon, plus
   wedges to serve
200g baby spinach
sea salt and black pepper

CLEVER COMBINATION:
The combination of onions, garlic and tomatoes is a powerful triple-whammy when it comes to heart health. Onions are rich in flavonoids that protect the inner lining of blood vessels from damage, garlic contains the anti-coagulant ajoene and tomatoes are rich in anti-inflammatory carotenoids.

Heat a little olive oil in a pan, add the onions and garlic and cook for 4–5 minutes, until softened. Add the tomatoes, olives and oregano, season with salt and pepper and simmer for about 10 minutes, until a thick, rich tomato sauce forms.

Preheat the oven to 200°C/400°F/Gas mark 6 and line a baking sheet with kitchen foil. Place the cod on the tray. Squeeze over half the lemon juice and season with salt and pepper. Bake for 15–20 minutes, until just cooked through.

Meanwhile, put the spinach in a steamer and steam until wilted.

Place the wilted spinach in the centre of a plate, put the cod fillet on top and smother it with the sauce. Drizzle with a little olive oil and serve with lemon wedges.

GOOD FOR: Type 2 diabetes, high blood pressure & high cholesterol

Coconut cod curry with fried brown basmati This is a great recipe for a wet Saturday evening, when you can take your time in the kitchen and enjoy all the wonderful aromas and textures while you cook it.

SERVES 4

olive oil, for cooking
1 onion, grated
2 teaspoons grated fresh
	ginger
2 red chillies, finely chopped,
	seeds left in
4 cloves garlic, finely chopped
2 large tomatoes, very finely
	chopped, any juice retained
2 teaspoons garam masala
½ teaspoon cumin seeds
1 teaspoon cinnamon
400ml coconut milk
200ml vegetable stock
4 large cod fillets
240g brown basmati rice
1 red onion, finely chopped
½ teaspoon turmeric
100g garden peas
sea salt and black pepper

Heat a little olive oil in a pan, add the onion, ginger, chillies and garlic and cook for 4–5 minutes, until it forms a dark paste. Add the tomatoes and any juice and cook for 5 minutes. Add the garam masala, cumin and cinnamon and cook for 2 more minutes. Add the coconut milk and stock, bring to the boil and add the cod. Simmer for 4–5 minutes, or until the cod has cooked through. Season with salt and pepper.

Meanwhile, cover the rice with boiling water and simmer for 20 minutes, or until just tender. Drain well. Heat a little olive oil in a pan, add the onion and cook for 4–5 minutes, until softened. Add the turmeric and peas and cook for a further 3 minutes. Add the cooked rice, season with salt and pepper and stir well.

Place a mound of the rice in the centre of each plate. Place the cod on top, cover with curry sauce and serve immediately.

STAR INGREDIENT: Brown basmati is at the top of the rice tree. It has the lowest glycaemic impact, so it maintains blood sugar slowly, helping stabilize energy levels and curb inflammation.

Nurturing nasi goreng The great thing about this gorgeous Indonesian rice dish is that you can throw anything in the pot. It's a great way of using leftover chicken or seafood, or any type of vegetable.

SERVES 4

250g brown rice
4 eggs
olive oil, for cooking
3 shallots, finely
　chopped
3 cloves garlic, finely
　chopped
3 spring onions,
　roughly chopped
1 red chilli, sliced,
　seeds left in
300g raw peeled prawns
3 tablespoons soy sauce
2 tablespoons chilli bean sauce
handful salted peanuts

Cover the rice with boiling water and simmer for 20 minutes, until just tender. Drain and set aside.

Crack the eggs into a bowl and whisk them lightly. Place a small pan over a medium heat, add the eggs and cook them as if you were making scrambled eggs, then set aside.

Heat a little olive oil in another pan, add the shallots, garlic, spring onions and chilli and cook for 4–5 minutes, until softened and beginning to turn translucent. Add the prawns and cook for 5–7 minutes, until cooked through. Stir in the rice until everything is well mixed.

Stir in the soy sauce and chilli bean sauce. Add the egg and gently fold it through. Serve immediately, garnished with peanuts.

CLEVER COMBINATION: The protein and complex carbohydrate in egg and brown rice respectively work together to help with insulin resistance, Type 2 diabetes and weight management issues.

Feel-good fish pie

I do love a good fish pie. Unfortunately, the traditional version can be a tad, well, rib-sticking. This is a lighter version with an extra nutritional boost. Using a ready-prepared fish pie mix, which are available in most supermarkets, makes it a lot easier.

SERVES 4

5 large sweet potatoes, peeled and cut into large chunks
olive oil, for cooking
1 onion, finely chopped
2 cloves garlic, finely chopped
400g low-fat cream cheese
200ml vegetable stock
1 tablespoon wholegrain mustard
600g fish pie mix
10g fresh dill, roughly chopped
sea salt and black pepper

STAR INGREDIENT:
Sweet potatoes are packed with beta carotene, which gives them their bright orange colour. It's a fat-soluble antioxidant that's very good for the skin, protecting collagen from damage and reducing inflammation and redness.

Put the sweet potatoes in a saucepan and cover with salted boiling water. Simmer for around 20 minutes, until very soft.

Meanwhile, preheat the oven to 200°C/400°F/ Gas mark 6. Heat a little olive oil in a pan, add the onion and garlic and cook for 4–5 minutes, until softened. Add the cream cheese, vegetable stock and mustard and cook gently over a medium heat, stirring, until the cheese has melted. Add the fish pie mix and simmer for 10 minutes, until the fish is nearly cooked through. Add the dill, season with salt and pepper and stir well.

Transfer the fish mixture to a baking dish. Drain and mash the sweet potato until smooth, then season with salt and pepper. Top the fish with the sweet potato mash and bake for about 15 minutes, until the sauce is bubbling and the top of the mash is starting to get crispy. Serve immediately, with a green salad or some steamed kale, broccoli or asparagus.

Green curry salmon burgers with edamame quinoa This oozes sophistication, looks stunning and is great for parties, plus you know it's going to be doing you real good. Edamame beans are available frozen in most supermarkets (they're sometimes called soya beans).

SERVES 4

4 skinless salmon fillets, cubed
2 cloves garlic, finely chopped
1–2 tablespoons Thai green
   curry paste
juice of 2 limes, plus
   wedges to serve
200g quinoa
150g edamame beans,
   thawed if frozen
large bunch fresh coriander,
   coarsely chopped, plus
   extra to garnish
olive oil, for frying
sea salt and black pepper

STAR INGREDIENT:
Coriander contains essential oils that can ease bloating and wind. Some experiments on animals have also suggested that compounds in coriander may help stimulate the release of insulin.

Place the salmon, garlic, curry paste and half the lime juice in a food processor, season with salt and process into a smooth, mince-like texture. Remove the mixture, divide in half, and, using your hands, form 4 burger-patty shapes. Set aside in the fridge to firm up slightly.

Meanwhile, place the quinoa in a saucepan, cover with boiling water and simmer for 10–15 minutes, or until just tender. Drain the quinoa and stir in the edamame beans, remaining lime juice and chopped coriander and season with salt and pepper. Stir well and set aside.

Heat a little olive oil in a frying pan, add the salmon burgers and fry for about 5 minutes on each side.

Place some quinoa in the centre of each plate (you could use a ring mould if you have one). Place the burger on top and garnish with a sprig of coriander and a lime wedge. Serve with a green salad, cooked broccoli or coleslaw.

Citrus salmon with garlicky pak choi

Citrus, garlic and soy together remind me of my old takeaway favourites, but this is super-tasty and super-healthy.

SERVES 4

olive oil, for cooking
1 onion, finely chopped
4 cloves garlic, finely chopped
juice of 3 oranges
juice of 1 lime
2 teaspoons grated lime zest
4 salmon fillets
500g pak choi, leaves
   separated
4 teaspoons soy sauce
2 teaspoons runny honey
sea salt and black pepper

STAR INGREDIENT:
Citrus fruits are famous for vitamin C, but they don't contain as much as you may think, and the amounts can be variable. However, another group of compounds that I'm really interested in are found in abundance here: the flavonoids. These are fantastic for the overall health of the cardiovascular system, as they help to strengthen the inner lining of blood vessels, making them more resilient to damage.

Preheat the oven to 200°C/400°F/Gas mark 6 and line a baking tray with kitchen foil. Heat a little olive oil in a small pan, add the onion and one of the garlic cloves and cook for 4–5 minutes, until softened. Add the orange and lime juice and zest and simmer gently until it has reduced by about half and has a thicker texture. Season with salt and pepper.

Place the salmon fillets on the baking sheet and bake for 15–20 minutes, until just cooked through.

Heat a little olive oil in another pan, add the pak choi and stir-fry for about 2 minutes. Add the remaining garlic, soy sauce and honey and continue to cook for another 2 minutes. Place the sautéed pak choi in the centre of a plate, put a salmon fillet on top and top with citrus sauce. Serve immediately, with some crushed new potatoes, if you like.

Cholesterol-busting chicken curry

Who doesn't love a good curry? This filling dish will quickly become a family teatime favourite, or a popular dish for sharing with friends – a one-pot wonder at its best. You could swap the chicken for fish, seafood or tofu.

SERVES 4

olive oil, for cooking
2 large red onions,
    finely chopped
6 cloves garlic,
    finely chopped
400g red lentils
800ml vegetable stock
6 skinless chicken breasts,
    cut into bite-sized pieces
2–3 tablespoons madras curry
    paste (or use a milder one)
300g baby spinach leaves
sea salt and black pepper
thick live probiotic yoghurt,
    to serve (optional)

Heat a little olive oil in a pan, add the onions and garlic and cook for 4–5 minutes, until softened. Add the lentils and a little of the stock and simmer. Keep adding small amounts of stock bit by bit as the lentils cook and soften, as if you were cooking a risotto.

Once the lentils are starting to soften and break down, add the chicken and curry paste and stir well. Continue simmering and adding the stock until the chicken has cooked through.

Add the baby spinach at the last minute, season with salt and pepper and stir until the spinach has wilted. Serve immediately, with a dollop of yoghurt on top, if you like.

STAR INGREDIENT: Have you noticed that red lentils break down when cooked? That's because they are very rich in soluble fibre, which is great for lowering cholesterol. It does this by binding to cholesterol in the bowel and carrying it away before it gets absorbed.

Chicken & feta calcium-booster

This is a light, protein-packed dish that's a great dinner party number, or just perfect for a quiet weekend lunch. The combination of spinach, dill and feta will take you back to your Greek holidays.

SERVES 4

500g baby spinach
4 large, boneless chicken
  breasts, skin on
2 tablespoons ricotta cheese
15g fresh dill, roughly chopped
100g feta cheese
sea salt and black pepper

CLEVER COMBINATION:
These ingredients create an almost perfect dish for skeletal and bone health. Feta, like all cheeses, is a good source of calcium, but calcium alone is not enough for healthy bones. We need magnesium, silica, boron and vitamin D to take the calcium into the bones. This recipe provides calcium, magnesium and vitamin D in one dish!

Preheat the oven to 200°C/400°F/Gas mark 6. Put the spinach in a steamer and steam for a few minutes, until wilted. Place in a colander, squeeze all the moisture out, then chop it finely.

Meanwhile, take the chicken breasts and slowly run your finger along the inside of the skin, separating the skin from the breast and creating a pocket. Make sure the skin stays attached to the chicken.

Transfer the spinach to a bowl with the ricotta and dill, and season with salt and pepper. Stir well. Crumble in the feta cheese and stir again gently.

Fill the space between the chicken skin and breast with the spinach and feta mixture. Place the chicken on a roasting tray and bake for about 20 minutes, or until the chicken is just cooked through. Serve with a tomato and cucumber salad and boiled new potatoes, if you like.

This slightly adjusted version of the summer classic, sangria, is great for parties, and when made like this can also be a great source of some very potent, healthful compounds. We need to have fun in life, and with a bit of creativity we can tick two boxes at once: enjoying ourselves and being good to our bodies.

GOOD FOR:
Cardiovascular health

GOOD FOR:
Blood vessel lining, reducing cholesterol oxidation

Sumptuous sangria

SERVES 3–4
300ml red wine
200ml blood orange juice
100ml pomegranate juice
1 large orange, sliced
ice cubes
fresh mint, to serve (optional)

Mix the wine and juices together in a large jug, add the sliced orange and chill in the fridge before adding the ice and serving. Add some fresh mint leaves just before serving, if you like.

STAR INGREDIENT: Red wine has long been linked with cardiovascular health benefits. One of the key compounds involved is resveratrol, which helps give wine its colour. This increases the production of nitric oxide by blood vessels, causing them to relax, and reduces the pressure within them. Resveratrol is also thought to reduce oxidation of bad (LDL) cholesterol and excessive clotting.

The deep blue

SERVES 1
1 green tea bag
150ml frozen blueberries
1 teaspoon runny honey
75ml vodka

Brew the green tea with 150ml boiling water in the same way you would if you were making a normal cuppa. Leave to cool down completely.

Place the blueberries, cold tea, honey and vodka in a blender and blitz into a thick, awesome, naughty smoothie.

STAR INGREDIENT: Blueberries contain a potent group of compounds called anthocyanins, which are also found in red wine. They are thought to offer protection against bad (LDL) cholesterol oxidation, and also protect the inner lining of blood vessels from damage.

Grape & cucumber skin-tingling spritzer This is a delightful summer drink, and a perfect accompaniment to a barbecue or picnic. It needs a juicer of some kind – a basic one is fine.

SERVES 6
500g seedless white grapes
2 cucumbers
1 bottle Prosecco

Pass the grapes and cucumbers through a juicer, and stir the juice well. Chill it in the fridge.

Half-fill a champagne flute with the juice and top up with Prosecco.

STAR INGREDIENT: Cucumbers are often thought of as somewhat dull in terms of nutritional value. However, they are one of the few decent dietary sources of silica, the mineral so important for smooth, healthy skin. In fact, it's silica that's responsible for the shiny skin on a cucumber. They also contain some interesting anti-inflammatory flavonoid compounds, too.

Healthy indulgence

Desserts and sweet treats tend to be a troublesome issue for those of us who want to eat healthily and try not to be naughty too often. It seems as though all the things we like are bad for us, and we worry about getting a spare tyre around the waist after the merest of mouthfuls.

Well, I'm a firm believer in not being a martyr in the name of health. We should be able to get pleasure and indulgence from our food – why on earth not? Food is a gift and should be enjoyed. The key is to get creative with how we prepare our treats and desserts, and to be smart about the ingredients we choose. Here's a bunch of sweets and desserts that feel really indulgent and will go down brilliantly with family and friends.

Avocado, lime & coconut crumble pots

These make for a beautifully refreshing and very virtuous little dessert or guilt-free snack at any time of day.

SERVES 4

2 large, very ripe avocados
grated zest and juice of 2 limes
3 tablespoons coconut oil,
   melted
3 teaspoons honey or agave
   nectar (syrup)
1 teaspoon desiccated coconut
8 low-sugar oat biscuits
4 teaspoons flaxseeds

Scoop out the flesh of the avocados and place in a bowl. Add the lime juice, coconut oil, honey and half the desiccated coconut and crush well until smooth (alternatively, you can process them in a blender).

Scoop the mixture into 4 small glasses or ramekins, making sure there's at least a 2cm gap at the top. Refrigerate for 2–4 hours.

When ready to serve, crumble the biscuits and sprinkle them over the top of each one, along with the reserved coconut, lime zest and some flaxseeds to make a crunchy layer. Serve immediately.

CLEVER COMBINATION: The ingredients come together to make this pretty much an essential fatty acid supplement. Coconut oil is rich in medium-chain triglycerides; avocados are rich in omega 3, 6 and 9; flaxseeds contain ALA omega 3.

Coconut panna cotta

I remember the first time I tried a vanilla panna cotta – it felt like a heavenly white chocolate whirlwind! But gallons of cream, sugar and gelatine mean that panna cotta is not the healthiest pudding out there. So here's a re-vamped version.

MAKES 4 SMALL OR 2 LARGE PANNA COTTAS

1 tablespoon agar agar
400ml coconut milk
1 vanilla pod
1 tablespoon stevia,
    or to taste (see below)
toasted coconut shavings,
    to serve (optional)
fresh raspberries,
    to serve (optional)

Dissolve the agar agar in 2 tablespoons water (check the instructions on the packet). Put the coconut milk in a pan. Split the vanilla pod in half and scrape out the seeds with the back of a knife, then add them to the coconut milk along with the stevia. Place the pan over a medium heat. Cook, stirring constantly, for 6 minutes. Add the agar agar mixture and keep stirring for another 2–3 minutes.

Pour into moulds such as small wine glasses or ramekins. Refrigerate for 4–6 hours. Serve on their own, or scattered with toasted coconut shavings and raspberries, if you like.

STAR INGREDIENT: Stevia is a plant-based sweetener that's truly benign. Many so-called healthy sweeteners claim to be completely harmless but send blood sugar levels sky high, so I see no benefit there. Stevia has no influence on blood sugar at all, which means we can finally enjoy sweetness without compromising our health. It's available in health food shops and some supermarkets. The sweetness of different brands varies, so you might need to adjust the quantity accordingly.

Berry-coconut ice lollies

The amount of sugar and grisly ingredients that go into shop-bought lollies makes the mind boggle, but these are clean, straightforward, nutrient-dense and taste delicious. Perfect for a sweet boost on a hot summer day.

MAKES 6
300g fresh blueberries
400ml coconut milk
150g live probiotic yoghurt
1 tablespoon runny honey
juice of ¼ lime

Place all the ingredients in a blender and process to a smooth purée. Pour into ice lolly moulds, add the lolly sticks and freeze overnight.

STAR INGREDIENT: Most of us have heard that coconut contains saturated fat. But saying that all saturated fat is bad for you is a bit like saying all cars are silver; in fact, they vary, and the fats in coconut are medium-chain triglycerides (MCT), which are broken down very quickly by enzymes secreted by the lining of the blood vessels, and can be used as an efficient energy source. That means they're very unlikely to be stored by the body or cause any problems in the cardiovascular system.

Sweet potato pie Sweet potatoes in a pie may seem strange, but it's traditional at Thanksgiving. I've made a version that tastes like heaven but is much better for you than the usual sugar bomb. Try bringing this out next time you have friends over for dinner!

SERVES 6

60g coconut oil, plus
   extra for greasing
2 large sweet potatoes
120g crushed mixed nuts
120g rolled oats
230g wholemeal flour
2 tablespoons maple syrup
   or agave nectar (syrup)
170ml almond milk
50g stevia (see page 145)
3 tablespoons cornflour
1 teaspoon ground nutmeg
1 teaspoon cinnamon
small pinch chilli powder

STAR INGREDIENT:
The rich orange flesh of
sweet potatoes comes from
beta carotene, which can
offer localized antioxidant
and anti-inflammatory
activity. They are also rich
in fibre, and their sugars
stimulate the growth of
good bacteria in the gut.

Preheat the oven to 200°C/400°F/Gas mark 6 and grease a 23cm round baking dish or tart tin with coconut oil. Put the sweet potatoes in the oven for about 1 hour, or until they are very soft all the way through. Once baked, scoop out the flesh and set aside to cool. Turn down the oven to 190°C/375°F/Gas mark 5.

Meanwhile, gently melt the coconut oil in a pan over a very low heat. Mix the crushed nuts, oats, flour, melted oil and maple syrup together in a bowl to form a crumbly, dough-like texture.

Press the mixture into the prepared baking dish or tart tin and bake for 25 minutes, or until golden brown. Remove and leave to cool.

Mix the sweet potato flesh, almond milk, stevia, cornflour and spices together and beat vigorously with a wooden spoon to create a smooth mixture. Fill the baked base with this mixture and return to the oven for a further hour. Leave to cool completely before serving.

Tofu berry layer
I know, I know. Putting tofu in a dessert sounds about as appealing as reading the phonebook in the rain. But have a little faith in me here! Silken tofu basically just creates a creamy carrier for whatever flavours you want to add.

SERVES 4

1 block silken tofu
   (usually around 350g)
300g fresh blueberries
300g fresh raspberries
1 tablespoon stevia
   (see page 145)
1 tablespoon runny
   honey, for drizzling

Place the tofu, half the blueberries, half the raspberries and the stevia in a blender and blitz into a deep purple-coloured creamy mixture.

Next, start layering the dish. Take a tall glass or bowl and place a layer of blueberries and raspberries in the bottom. Put a layer of the creamy berry tofu mixture on top, then repeat until the glass has filled. Chill in the fridge before serving drizzled with a little honey.

STAR INGREDIENT: If you eat tofu as it comes, it tastes like wet pencil rubber. But it allows us to create textures that are usually only achievable with slightly naughtier ingredients – it offers creaminess with no trans fats or sugar. It's a reasonable protein source and contains loads of calcium, too.

GOOD FOR: Skin health, high blood pressure, high cholesterol & blood vessel health

Bangin' berry tart This awesome dessert reminds me of a rather naughty version from a well-known London patisserie. It's fresh, vibrant, sweet and tart, easy to make, and best of all, absolutely nutrient packed.

SERVES 6

- 80ml olive oil, plus extra for greasing
- 230g rolled oats
- 60g almonds
- 60g walnuts
- 230g wholemeal flour
- 1 teaspoon cinnamon
- 2 tablespoons maple syrup
- 200g fresh blueberries
- 200g fresh blackberries
- 2 teaspoons stevia (see page 145)
- thick live probiotic yoghurt, to serve

STAR INGREDIENT:
Purple berries are among the healthiest fruits, thanks to the anthocyanins that create their deep purple colour, which are great for circulation. They're taken up by the cells that line the blood vessels, encouraging them to make nitric oxide, which helps the blood vessel walls relax, reducing pressure.

Preheat the oven to 200°C/400°F/Gas mark 6 and grease a 23cm tart tin with olive oil. Make the tart case by putting the oats, almonds and walnuts in a blender or food processor and blitzing to make a coarse, flour-like texture. Add the flour, cinnamon, olive oil and maple syrup to form a soft dough. Press it into the base of the tart tin. Bake for 20 minutes, or until golden brown and firm. Set aside and cool.

Meanwhile, put the blueberries and blackberries in a saucepan along with 2 tablespoons water and the stevia. Simmer over a medium-high heat for 30–40 minutes. This constant simmering will make the fruit break down and start to take on a jam-like texture, without the need to add thickeners. Carefully pour the filling into the cooled tart base, and chill for 4 hours. Serve with a good dollop of yoghurt on the side.

Winding down

There's a lot of comfort and feel-good factor in having a snack before bed. But there's a functional element, too. We know that certain foods can affect brain chemistry: some can make us feel relaxed, while others can make us feel stimulated and edgy. If you like having a little bedtime snack, choosing foods that will help you nod off and avoiding those that will keep you awake into the wee hours will help you get a good night's sleep. The ones to avoid are sugary snacks that create sharp rises in blood sugar, which is the opposite of what you need at this time of day.

Bedtime brew This will give you total knock-out in minutes. You can find valerian in your local health food shop.

SERVES 1

1 mug cows' milk
1 chamomile tea bag
2 teaspoons cocoa powder
20 drops valerian tincture

Pour the milk into a small pan. Add the tea bag and simmer gently for about 8–10 minutes, to make a milky chamomile infusion.

Put the cocoa powder in the mug and mix with a small amount of water to make a thick paste.

Remove the tea bag from the milk, squeezing it to release the last remnants of chamomile infusion. Add the valerian tincture and pour the hot milk into the mug, stirring well to mix it with the cocoa paste. Drink it 10 minutes before you go to bed.

CLEVER COMBINATION: This is a cocktail of potent ingredients that help promote sleep in several ways. Milk's calcium content can have a calming effect on the central nervous system, and its lactose can release endorphins. It's also rich in the amino acid tryptophan, which is turned into serotonin, the neurotransmitter that (among other things) regulates the body clock. Chamomile and valerian are both very relaxing herbs, too. Chamomile can calm the central nervous system, as can valerian, which is also a muscle relaxant.

GOOD FOR: Eczema & skin health, sleep problems & insomnia, heart health, workout & muscle recovery

Shut-eye sandwich This is great for easing you into a good night's sleep if you prefer a savoury snack.

SERVES 1
½ ripe avocado
juice of ½ lemon
½ wholemeal English muffin
3 slices cooked turkey breast
1 sprig fresh dill (optional)
sea salt and black pepper

Scoop out the avocado flesh into a bowl, add the lemon juice and season with salt and pepper. Mash with a fork to give a guacamole-like texture.

Toast the muffin half. Place the mashed avocado on the toasted muffin and top with the turkey slices and some fresh dill leaves, if you like.

CLEVER COMBINATION: Turkey isn't only a lean protein source – it's also one of the richest sources of the amino acid tryptophan, which is turned into the neurotransmitter serotonin. One of serotonin's major roles is to regulate sleep patterns, as it can be transformed into another neurotransmitter called melatonin, which induces sleep. Tryptophan needs to be eaten with a complex carbohydrate to give a subtle rise in insulin to catapult the tryptophan into the brain, so the wholemeal muffin provides the leg-up it needs.

Banana-peanut bagel This super-simple bedtime snack made with tryptophan-rich bananas is a quick, easy and effective way to combat hunger pangs, and won't keep you up all night.

SERVES 1

1 very ripe banana
½ wholemeal bagel
1 tablespoon natural
   crunchy peanut butter

Peel the banana and mash it well in a bowl. Toast the bagel.

Spread the peanut butter on top of the bagel and top with the mashed banana.

STAR INGREDIENT: Peanut butter contains the mineral magnesium, which can help relax the muscles and work as a mild relaxant to the central nervous system.

Mediterranean melatonin houmous

Houmous really is my kryptonite, and it makes a pretty awesome bedtime snack too. Make it in bulk and keep it in the fridge for late-night snack attacks.

SERVES 1

1 x 400g tin chickpeas,
   drained
juice of ½ lemon
4 tablespoons olive oil
1 clove garlic, crushed
1 bunch fresh basil,
   leaves torn
sea salt and black pepper

Place all the ingredients in a blender or food processor, season with salt and pepper and blend into a thick, luscious dip. Serve with an oatcake or celery sticks.

CLEVER COMBINATION: Chickpeas are rich in vitamin B6, which is important for the production of melatonin, the sleep hormone. Along with basil, which has been used for centuries in Western herbal medicine as a mild sedative, they create the perfect sleep-boosting snack.

The food pharmacy

The food we eat is so much more than merely fuel. It directly affects the internal biochemical terrain of the body. Every chemical reaction in every cell in every tissue in every system of the body uses nutrients in one form or another. Nutrient intake is about far more than just the well-known deficiency diseases such as scurvy and pellagra. It can have a direct impact on our susceptibility to disease, and our ability to fight it and recover from it. Thanks to the extent to which they can affect our physiology, nutrients are basically pharmaceutical agents.

The story doesn't end there, though. Nutrients – in other words, the components of our food that are essential to normal functioning – are only one part of the picture. There are many other compounds in our food that are not nutrients per se (because they're not essential for normal function), but can still directly affect our physiology. Many can even deliver a pharmacological effect. These extra components are the phytochemicals, compounds found in plants during normal growth and metabolism. There are thousands of these compounds, but some of them have stood out as potential heroes in the quest for better health.

This section provides an introduction to what is in your food and how it can affect you. It's an overview of what the different vitamins, minerals, fats and phytochemicals do, and which foods are richest in them. The list of nutrient sources are by no means exhaustive – I've just given you the best ones. I want to bring to your attention the vast and amazing array of powerful compounds in normal, everyday foods. I hope you'll be able to see for yourself the benefit of keeping it healthy every day!

VITAMINS

VITAMIN A

Vitamin A comes in two main forms: retinol and carotenoids (or carotenes). It is a fat-soluble nutrient that, in its two forms, is found in quite a diverse range of foods. Retinol is found in animal products such as meat and dairy, whereas carotenoids are the colour pigments found in plants and tend to account for red, yellow and orange colours in foods, such as the vivid orange of carrots and sweet potatoes. It is one of the most vital nutrients in our diet and supports important aspects of the body's metabolism.

WHAT YOU NEED IT FOR
Antioxidant protection
Eyesight
Immune function
Gene manufacture
Healthy skin
Reproduction & menstrual cycle

WHERE YOU'LL FIND IT
Retinol: Butter, liver, red meat, whole milk
Carotenoids: Carrots, green leafy vegetables,
  mangoes, red peppers, sweet potatoes

VITAMIN B1 (THIAMIN)

Thiamin was first discovered in the late 1800s, when sailors in Asia who were eating a staple diet of white rice began displaying signs of the disease associated with B1 deficiency: beriberi. When some of the white rice was replaced with brown rice, meat and vegetables, the symptoms went away. Symptoms of low B1 include mental fatigue and confusion, and severe beriberi consists of acute episodes of this coupled with muscle wasting. Thiamin is a B vitamin that is easily leached from the body, and is almost non-existent in processed foods, and because of this it's a nutrient that is commonly lacking in many people.

WHAT YOU NEED IT FOR
Carbohydrate metabolism
Energy production
Nerve cell activity

WHERE YOU'LL FIND IT
Seeds
Soya beans
Whole grains

VITAMIN B2 (RIBOFLAVIN)

Riboflavin forms part of a yellowish pigment in foods, and it's what's responsible for the tell-tale fluorescent laser urine you get when taking multivitamins and B complex supplements. B2 is one of the most important nutrients for helping convert glucose to energy inside our cells.

WHAT YOU NEED IT FOR
Carbohydrate metabolism
Cellular protection and enhancing cells' natural
  defences (it increases glutathione, an enzyme that
  breaks down and removes waste products from cells)
Energy production

WHERE YOU'LL FIND IT
Almonds
Liver
Mushrooms
Whole grains

VITAMIN B3 (NIACIN)

Niacin is a B vitamin that some people don't consider to be essential because our body can manufacture it by itself. It is important in helping to manage increasingly prevalent conditions such as high cholesterol and diabetes, however, and I believe there is an increased need for it in our diets that is unlikely to be met by the body alone. It's the precursor for (in other words, it helps with the creation of) several enzymes and co-enzymes that are responsible for some of the most important cellular metabolic activities in the body. In the eighteenth century, it was discovered that niacin deficiency was the cause of the awful disease pellagra.

WHAT YOU NEED IT FOR
Blood sugar regulation
Cholesterol reduction
Detoxification processes
Energy production

WHERE YOU'LL FIND IT
Almonds
Brown rice
Peanuts
Pine nuts
Yeast

VITAMIN B5 (PANTOTHENIC ACID)

Pantothenic acid is another vital component in cellular metabolism and the production of energy from dietary glucose. It helps produce a substance called co-enzyme A, which is a key component in cells for converting glucose into ATP (adenosine triphosphate), which powers every cell in our body. It is one of the most widely occurring nutrients, so deficiency is unlikely.

WHAT YOU NEED IT FOR

Cellular energy production
Cholesterol reduction
Regulation & production of adrenal hormones
Utilization of dietary fats

WHERE YOU'LL FIND IT

Broccoli
Fish
Offal
Poultry
Sweet potatoes

VITAMIN B6 (PYRIDOXINE)

This vital B vitamin is a key nutrient for the production and maintenance of structural compounds and proteins. It regulates the production of compounds involved in managing the inflammatory response, regulates immunity and red blood cell function. Deficiency can cause depression, fatigue and anaemia-like symptoms, but for me its most important role is in cardiovascular health, as it can help regulate blood pressure by balancing sodium and potassium. It also reduces levels of homocysteine, a potential cause of cardiovascular problems.

WHAT YOU NEED IT FOR

Asthma management
Blood sugar control & diabetes management
Cardiovascular health
Energy production
Healthy nervous system
Mind & mood
Regulating immunity

WHERE YOU'LL FIND IT

Bananas
Beans & pulses
Brown rice
Brussels sprouts

VITAMIN B12 (COBALAMIN)

Vitamin B12 is another one that's never far from the headlines, and is very familiar to vegetarians, who can struggle to get it in their diet adequately. For vegans, supplementation is their only option. There are many claims that certain plant foods contain usable B12, but unfortunately it's difficult to absorb them. The elderly also struggle with B12, as its absorption relies on something called intrinsic factor, which requires stomach acid for its production. The elderly have reduced stomach acid, so intrinsic factor levels soon begin to decline. Deficiency can cause fatigue, pernicious anaemia and nervous system problems. It's stored in the liver and it can take up to six years for the levels to deplete before deficiency signs begin to show.

WHAT YOU NEED IT FOR

Cardiovascular health
Nerve cell function
Red blood cell manufacture & development

WHERE YOU'LL FIND IT

Cheese
Eggs
Fish
Offal

BIOTIN

Biotin is also vital for cellular metabolism. It's involved in producing fatty acids and is important in gluconeo-genesis, the process of creating glucose/ATP from non-glucose sources; when there is little glucose available, the body can produce it from fatty acids and amino acids. Even a slight biotin deficiency can cause unpleasant side effects such as skin problems and hair loss. As well as getting it from food, the bacteria in our digestive system can manufacture biotin.

WHAT YOU NEED IT FOR

Cell growth
Metabolism of macronutrients (such as fats, sugars
   & amino acids)
Sebaceous gland function

WHERE YOU'LL FIND IT

Eggs
Mushrooms
Nuts
Wheat

CHOLINE

Choline is one of the lesser-known B-group vitamins, but it's a vitally important one for the brain and nervous system. It's a nutrient that can be synthesized in the body, but its importance for fat metabolism and mental functions have caused it to become classed as essential. It is a vital component in maintaining the structure of cell membranes, especially nerve cells, and regulating communication across cell membranes.

WHAT YOU NEED IT FOR

Fat metabolism
Liver function
Memory
Mood stability

WHERE YOU'LL FIND IT

Beans
Cauliflower
Eggs (especially the yolks)
Liver

FOLIC ACID

Folic acid is definitely the best known of the B vitamins, and it's the one that has been the focus of many headlines, public health campaigns and debates. It is most widely known for its role in the development of the neural tube in a developing foetus, and a deficiency of it can cause spina bifida. Its role extends much further than this, though. It is a vital nutrient for the manufacture of DNA and DNA repair.

WHAT YOU NEED IT FOR

Cardiovascular health
Cellular growth & division
DNA synthesis
Homocysteine reduction
Mood stability & depression

WHERE YOU'LL FIND IT

Asparagus
Beans
Broccoli
Green leafy vegetables
Sweet potatoes

VITAMIN C

Vitamin C is the biggest-selling nutritional supplement in the world, and has been the centre of many debates and much research in Europe and the US. It is incredible how a single nutrient can gain such a cult following and be promoted as such a universal panacea. It is, though, one of the most important vitamins in human nutrition, and is so much more than just a potential treatment for the winter sniffles. It first came to light when sailors fell plague to scurvy during long voyages, with very few food choices in their ships' holds. It was only when, in the late eighteenth century, the likes of Captain Cook and his crew remained scurvy-free on voyages where limes and berries were plentiful that the connection was made. The British Navy began carrying limes aboard all vessels – hence the nickname 'limeys'. Many reasons were suggested for why limes and fruit kept scurvy at bay, but it was soon discovered that vitamin C was the magic bullet.

Over the years, many claims have been made for vitamin C, whether it's obtained from foods or supplements. Some of these are quite sensible and logical, whereas others are downright weird and absurd. Many trials have tried to investigate whether vitamin C intake can influence things such as the common cold, or even cardiovascular health, but the answers remain unclear and the debate continues. However, there does seem to be some logic behind the argument for vitamin C and immunity, since it increases what's known as the 'oxidative burst' from white blood cells. This is a sudden burst of highly reactive free-radical compounds that white blood cells use to destroy pathogens and bugs.

WHAT YOU NEED IT FOR

Collagen production
Immune support
Wound healing

WHERE YOU'LL FIND IT

Berries
Citrus fruits
Peppers
Spinach

VITAMIN D

Vitamin D has been all over the international press in recent years, and understandably so. It has been the centre of a great deal of research, and some of the things that have been revealed about this vitamin are staggering – they could easily fill a book on their own. It has been known for a long time that vitamin D had a vital role to play in the regulation of calcium, from maintaining serum calcium concentrations through to transporting calcium into the skeleton. However, recent revelations have shown that it has a role to play in mental and emotional functions, immune regulation, even fat metabolism and protection against some cancers. The primary source for humans is the conversion of cholesterol into vitamin D precursors when our skin is exposed to ultraviolet radiation from the sun. So those of us in cold climates are in trouble! No wonder we all feel so rotten when the sun disappears. Thankfully, there are a few food sources as well.

WHAT YOU NEED IT FOR
Immunological support
Mental & emotional health
Skeletal health
Systemic calcium regulation

WHERE YOU'LL FIND IT
Eggs
Milk (whole)
Mushrooms
Oily fish

VITAMIN E

Vitamin E is another nutrient that virtually everyone has heard of, and one that has dominated the beauty product industry for decades. Its primary role is as an antioxidant against lipid-derived free radicals (highly reactive by-products in the body, which can cause great damage to cells and tissues), and also to protect fatty structures in the body. It gets incorporated into the fatty membranes of our cells, where it can offer some protection to these fatty structures against certain types of damage. It is especially important for the health of the skin in this context. It also works in tandem with vitamin A and vitamin C to offer broad-spectrum antioxidant protection. Vitamin E is known to have an anticoagulant activity, too.

WHAT YOU NEED IT FOR
Antioxidant function
Cardiovascular health
Cell membrane protection
Skin health & scarring

WHERE YOU'LL FIND IT
Almonds
Avocados
Olive oil

MINERALS & TRACE ELEMENTS

BORON

The importance of boron in human health was debated for many many years. We now know that it plays an important role in the maintenance of skeletal health by regulating the activity of vitamin D, and also reducing calcium loss from the body.

WHAT YOU NEED IT FOR
Skeletal health

WHERE YOU'LL FIND IT
Most fruits & vegetables

CALCIUM

Calcium is the most talked-about mineral – greatly misunderstood, and certainly over-prescribed. I can't think of anyone who wouldn't automatically think of strong, healthy bones when asked about calcium, so many people guzzle down huge amounts of calcium in the hope of keeping bones healthy. However, in my opinion, calcium is actually the least important part of the picture when it comes to bone health. I use the analogy of calcium being just like the bricks and cement on a building site. Yes, it is the structural material that the skeleton is built from. But without a team of builders (in this case, auxiliary nutrients such as vitamin D, magnesium, boron and so on), nothing will get built. Its importance has been exaggerated over the years. The other big myth is that when it comes to dietary calcium, it's always dairy products first. Granted, these are great sources, but not everyone wants to, or is able to, consume them. There are many rich plant sources, too.

WHAT YOU NEED IT FOR
Cellular communication
Muscular contraction
Strengthening bones

WHERE YOU'LL FIND IT
Cabbage
Cashew nuts
Dairy products
Kale
Sesame seeds

CHROMIUM

This trace element has become a bit of a buzz nutrient in recent years, especially in the natural products industry. I suspect that's mostly due to its main function, which feels very relevant to modern life and the array of dietary health issues it presents. Chromium's main role is to form Glucose Tolerance Factor, which helps with blood sugar control and the regulation of glucose activity. One of the biggest issues relating to the modern Western diet is something called metabolic syndrome, which features high blood pressure, high cholesterol, abdominal weight gain and chronic fatigue. This is caused by the body's lack of responsiveness to the hormone insulin. Additional chromium in the diet may help with insulin resistance, although the results of studies have been mixed. What we do know for certain is the physiological role of chromium, so getting it into the diet is always a good idea.

WHAT YOU NEED IT FOR
Blood sugar control
Insulin regulation

WHERE YOU'LL FIND IT
Meats
Whole grains

COPPER

Often overlooked, this trace element is involved in some key chemical reactions in the body, and is found in high concentrations in the liver and brain. It's important for iron absorption and skeletal health.

WHAT YOU NEED IT FOR
Healthy bones & teeth
Skin health

WHERE YOU'LL FIND IT
Beans
Oysters
Prawns

MAGNESIUM

Magnesium has been the focus of a massive amount of research in recent years, and is considered a vital nutrient for the health of virtually every body system. Since it's the second most highly concentrated mineral in the body, and is involved in more than 1,000 enzymatic reactions, this comes as no surprise. Essential for skeletal health, muscular relaxation, cardiovascular health and neurological health, this commonly deficient nutrient should not be overlooked, and it's green foods all the way here. Chlorophyll in plants has basically the same structure as haemoglobin (the protein in red blood cells that carries oxygen, which is taken into our tissues) in humans. Haemoglobin contains four iron units within it, whereas chlorophyll contains four magnesium units. So, the greener the plant, the higher the magnesium.

WHAT YOU NEED IT FOR

Blood pressure reduction
Cellular communication
Energy production
Protein synthesis
Muscular relaxation

WHERE YOU'LL FIND IT

Beans
Green vegetables
Tofu
Whole grains

POTASSIUM

Potassium is one of the main electrolytes (charged minerals involved in cellular communication and fluid regulation) in the body, and it's important for regulating a massive array of cellular responses. It is involved in regulating blood pressure, neurological functions and heart function, to name but a few of its vital roles. Potassium works alongside sodium and chloride, and one of the issues of the modern Western diet is that many of us are consuming way more sodium than potassium. This can lead to water retention and a hardening of the blood vessels, leading to increased blood pressure and increased risk of damage to the vessel walls. More potassium than sodium generally has the opposite effect. The ideal scenario is a balance between the two.

WHAT YOU NEED IT FOR

Blood pressure regulation
Cellular communication
Nerve cell function

WHERE YOU'LL FIND IT

Bananas
Carrots
Oranges

ZINC

I believe zinc is one of the most important nutrients of all. It's found in every cell in the body and is involved in more biochemical processes than any other mineral, such as the production of enzymes that break down and remove potentially harmful compounds from our cells, and also remove waste materials. It regulates taste, smell and sex hormones such as testosterone. Many clinical trials have shown that zinc is one nutrient that definitely helps prevent and treat the common cold. It's used by white blood cells to code specific genes, including those that control the way cells respond to certain stimuli and pathogens. Zinc is also top of my list for treating acne because it regulates the sebaceous (oil-secreting) glands in the skin, and its action in white blood cells helps clear infection.

WHAT YOU NEED IT FOR

Acne
Eczema
Hormonal regulation
Immune support
Normal cell growth
Oily skin

WHERE YOU'LL FIND IT

Beans
Meats
Nuts
Oily fish
Prawns
Pumpkin seeds

FATS & FATTY ACIDS

OMEGA 3

Omega-3 fatty acids are a group of essential good fats with a wide range of health benefits. There are three forms of omega 3: EPA, DHA and ALA. EPA is a powerful natural inflammatory mediator; DHA is more of a structural fatty acid and is vital for the production and maintenance of the myelin sheath, the fatty outer membrane of nerve cells; ALA is the plant form of omega 3, and is nowhere near as metabolically active as EPA and DHA, so it needs to be converted into these. Humans are not good at doing this, which is why it's best to get omega 3 from fish. Omega-3 supplements vary considerably and it's always worth getting one with the highest EPA levels you can find.

EPA

This omega-3 fatty acid is considered the Rolls Royce of natural inflammatory mediators. It's basically the metabolic building blocks of the body's own inherent anti-inflammatory chemicals, a group of very powerful compounds called prostaglandins. Some prostaglandins switch inflammation on and enhance pain signalling and muscular contraction (think menstrual or digestive cramps), whereas others reduce inflammation and pain signalling. They require fatty acids for their manufacture, and different fatty acids will deliver a different end product – a different class of prostaglandins. EPA helps the body to manufacture a class of prostaglandins known as series 3 or PGE3, which are powerfully anti-inflammatory. By increasing our intake of EPA, we greatly encourage the body to produce PGE3, thus helping manage inflammatory episodes within the body. This makes omega 3 a vital consideration for issues such as acne and eczema, in which EPA can reduce redness; arthritis, in which EPA can reduce pain and stiffness; and heart disease, in which EPA can reduce the inflammatory damage to blood vessels that can lead to atheroma (blockage of the arteries). It also helps increase good (HDL) and lower bad (LDL) cholesterol.

WHAT YOU NEED IT FOR
Acne & eczema
Arthritis
Heart disease

WHERE YOU'LL FIND IT
Brazil nuts
Mackerel
Salmon
Sunflower seeds

DHA

DHA is basically a structural fatty acid. It's one of the single most important dietary fats for the maintenance of the myelin sheath, the fatty substance that surrounds nerve cells, which are vital for proper nerve signalling. DHA is also an important structural component in the skin and the eyes. DHA is one of the single most important nutrients for a mother to take in during pregnancy and breastfeeding, as it plays a pivotal role in brain and neurological development. Some studies have shown that DHA intake may have potential relevance for both the prevention and management of certain disorders of the brain and nervous system. Some evidence suggests that high DHA intakes are associated with a reduced risk of Alzheimer's disease and Parkinson's disease. Evidence also indicates that DHA intake may ease depression in Parkinson's patients, and some studies have shown that DHA can positively influence plaque formation in Alzheimer's disease, although other trials found no effect.

DHA doesn't have the potent anti-inflammatory activity of EPA, but a new class of compounds called resolvins, which are metabolites of EPA and DHA, have been discovered (metabolites are substances produced by metabolism). These compounds can actually cause a local reversal of inflammatory events, and so may help to resolve the issue.

WHAT YOU NEED IT FOR
Cell membrane structure & maintenance
Reduction of inflammation that's already active

WHERE YOU'LL FIND IT
Algae
Seafood & oily fish

ALA

ALA is the plant-derived form of omega 3, found in foods such as flaxseeds and walnuts. While there are some health benefits associated with ALA, it's really the poor cousin of EPA and DHA. Why? Because we need to convert it into EPA and DHA first, using a whole selection of enzymatic processes. Some animals, such as salmon, are fabulous at doing this. Human beings are not; in fact we're dreadful at it. We manage to convert a tiny percentage of dietary ALA into EPA and DHA – perhaps 12 per cent, if that. Many people, usually those defending dietary ideals or commercial interests, will tell you that many of the properties associated with EPA and DHA (such as anti-inflammatory activity, effects on mood and neurological functions) can be gained from ALA. Alas, this simply isn't the case, and tomes of data back this up. We just don't convert it effectively enough. To get those effects, you need EPA and DHA, and they come from dietary sources such as oily fish and seafood. But that said, there are some definite links between ALA intake and improved cardiovascular health outcomes.

WHAT YOU NEED IT FOR
In theory, the same issues as EPA, but the action is far, far weaker because so much less is converted.

WHERE YOU'LL FIND IT
Flaxseeds & oil
Walnuts
Rapeseed oil

OMEGA 6

The omega-6 fatty acids were deemed 'essential' based on early investigations using animal subjects. However, these initial investigations had flawed methodology; they involved feeding rats an omega-6 deficient diet, but the oils they removed from the diet also contained omega 3. So the researchers had also potentially created omega 3 deficiency, which means their conclusions about omega 6 are now being called into question. Omega-6 fatty acids certainly are very metabolically active; many of their metabolic by-products are involved in pathological states, and are even targets for pharmaceutical drugs. They can also be metabolized to form a fatty acid called arachidonic acid, which can be turned into a communication molecule called a series-2 prostaglandin (PGE2), which stimulates and exacerbates inflammation. Many of the common anti-inflammatory drugs prescribed for conditions such as arthritis actually block the enzyme that converts arachidonic acid into PGE2. Omega-6 fatty acids also compete with omega-3 fatty acids for enzymes, which can affect the formation of the positive metabolic by-products of omega 3. However, one omega-6 fatty acid, GLA, can deliver some mild inflammation reduction and protection to cell membranes. But the amount you need is tiny compared with omega 3.

WHERE YOU'LL FIND IT
Nuts
Seeds
Vegetable oils

MCTS (MEDIUM-CHAIN TRIGLYCERIDES)

MCTs are another class of interesting dietary fats. They have a very specific size compared with other dietary fats, which means that they are rapidly absorbed and used. They are a very easy-to-use energy source for the body (they're often included in infant formulas and hospital feeds). As a result, they are far less likely to be stored, and certainly aren't around long enough to cause problems for the cardiovascular system. There are many claims that MCTs can actually cause the body to burn fat. I have reservations about this, since that will very much depend on the general composition of the person's diet. However, it is readily used for energy, so if you use it for cooking, you will burn more than you store, by default. So, from that point of view it is a good choice for those trying to watch their waistlines, but don't be fooled by marketing.

Some MCTs have an antiviral activity. The cream of the crop here is an MCT called caprylic acid. Some studies have shown that it has that action because it binds to a structure on the outer surface of viruses called the lipid-protein envelope. This is the mechanism that viruses use to enter cells and instigate infection. What isn't clear is if caprylic acid will deliver the same benefits when ingested orally, as these studies have all involved in-vitro testing.

WHAT YOU NEED THEM FOR
Heart health
Energy boost

WHERE YOU'LL FIND THEM
Coconut oil

PHYTONUTRIENTS

CAROTENOIDS

Carotenoids are a very widely distributed group of phytochemicals, primarily colour pigments in plants. In the body, carotenoids mostly deliver antioxidant activity. They are fat-soluble compounds, so they can accumulate in fatty tissues such as the subcutaneous layer of the skin. They do this so rapidly that people who eat a lot of carotenoid-rich foods can develop an orange tinge to the skin, which is called hypercarotenaemia. There is a big benefit here, though. When these compounds accumulate in the skin they can offer localized protection to the surrounding structures such as collagen and elastin fibres, and the pilosebaceous unit (the area where the hair follicle and sebaceous gland meet – this is the area that becomes inflamed when a spot forms). Essentially, this can have an anti-ageing effect.

Carotenoids also have an anti-inflammatory activity. Again, when they accumulate in tissues such as the skin, they can deliver a localized anti-inflammatory activity. This is great for issues such as eczema, acne and psoriasis, which all involve redness and inflammation. They are also useful for inflammatory problems in the digestive tract.

Carotenoids also have a reputation for benefiting eye and prostate health. Lutein, a yellow-coloured carotenoid, can accumulate in the macula densa of the eye, where it offers some protection against macular degeneration. The carotenoid lycopene, found in tomatoes, is believed to offer protection against prostate issues such as prostatic hyperplasia, and even prostate cancer. While there is debate around this, epidemiological data certainly does show an association between tomato intake and reduced prostate cancer risk. However, direct cause-and -effect relationships are yet to be confirmed.

WHAT YOU NEED THEM FOR
Acne
Eczema
Psoriasis
Reduced skin ageing
Skin health

WHERE YOU'LL FIND THEM
Carrots
Mangoes
Melons
Peppers
Spinach
Tomatoes

FLAVONOIDS

There are over 6,000 plant chemicals in the flavonoid family, which makes them one of the single most ubiquitous substances in our diets. The best-known flavonoids are anthocyanins, flavanols, flavonols, flavanones, flavones and isoflavones. They are responsible for colour pigments in plants, predominantly in shades of red, yellow and orange. They are a widely studied, powerful group of compounds with a range of health benefits. Probably the best example of their protective activity is in cardiovascular health. They are known to protect blood vessels from damage, reduce cholesterol oxidation, lower blood pressure and reduce clotting factors. They also deliver antioxidant and anti-inflammatory functions.

Many flavonoids have a wide array of protective functions against some serious health conditions. They are known to influence various cell signalling pathways. This has been suggested as one of the ways in which flavonoids can improve cognitive function, and even offer some protection against certain forms of cancers.

Flavonoids also stimulate the activity of enzymes in our cells that are responsible for general 'housekeeping'. They break down and remove certain toxins and metabolic waste products, keeping cells healthy.

WHAT YOU NEED THEM FOR
Heart health
Cognitive function
Reducing cholesterol
Reducing blood pressure
Anti-inflammatory

WHERE YOU'LL FIND THEM
Anthocyanins: blueberries red grapes, red wine
Flavanols: apples, chocolate, green tea
Flavanones: citrus fruit
Flavonols: berries, kale, onions
Flavones: celery, parsley, thyme
Isoflavones: seeds, soya products
General: cabbage, green tea, raspberries, red onions, red peppers, red wine, strawberries

GLUCOSINOLATES

Glucosinolates are compounds commonly found in vegetables from the *Brassica* family (such as cabbage, broccoli and kale), and are becoming points of interest for a great deal of research. They are made from glucose and amino acids, and are responsible for the bitter taste in foods like Brussels sprouts. Recent research has revealed that glucosinolates can cause a powerful stimulation of phase-2 enzymes. These are the enzymes in cells that can break down metabolic waste, and also disarm potential carcinogens. There is also some evidence to suggest that they can induce apoptosis (programmed cell death) in tumour cells.

WHAT YOU NEED THEM FOR
Cellular health & wellbeing

WHERE YOU'LL FIND THEM
Broccoli
Brussels sprouts
Cauliflower
Kale

POLYSACCHARIDES

Polysaccharides are basically a type of sugar. Not simple sugars like glucose or fructose, which are readily absorbed and used for energy – these are very large, high molecular-weight sugars that are very often not absorbed at all, or only partially broken down. Despite not being absorbed, some of these special sugars can deliver some profound health benefits.

The most widely researched, and in my opinion most exciting, effect they have is on immunological health. More than 40 years of clinical research from Japan and the US has shown that polysaccharides derived from mushrooms such as shiitake and maitake can notably increase white blood cell count. It was once thought that mushroom polysaccharides were digested and absorbed, and could directly affect tissues involved in white cell production. However, once it was discovered that these polysaccharides exit the body untouched, their true action was discovered. They deliver their effects by interacting with areas of tissue in the walls of the digestive tract called peyers patches. Peyers patches are basically like immunological surveillance stations, which constantly monitor gut contents and deliver information back to the immune system.

When you think about it, the digestive tract is an easy way in for would-be disease-causing agents, so these tissues need to be highly accurate and specialized. There are hundreds of cells within these patches, which basically communicate with the rest of the immune system, telling it what's going on and alerting it to attack. These cells can identify different types of pathogen or challenge and activate the relevant immunological response. When the polysaccharides from mushrooms come into contact with these patches of tissue, all hell breaks loose, a major alarm signal is raised by the cells in the surveillance stations, and a chemical cascade causes the body to start making more white cells. What causes this? Well, we have recently found out that mushroom polysaccharides are extraordinarily similar in structure to sugars that are found on the outside of bacterial cells. So, the body thinks it is under major attack and goes into defence mode. You can see how this would be beneficial during times of infection. The white cells are the soldiers of our immune system. So, having a temporarily heightened number of these can help us to fight infection faster.

The second major area of interest in terms of polysaccharides and health is cardiovascular health. Certain types of polysaccharides found in foods such as oats have been clinically proven to lower cholesterol. This is because when they're in the digestive tract, they form a gel-like texture that can help carry cholesterol away and out of the digestive tract before it gets absorbed.

WHAT YOU NEED THEM FOR
Cardiovascular health
Fighting infection
Immunological health

WHERE YOU'LL FIND THEM
Maitake mushrooms
Oats
Oyster mushrooms
Shiitake mushrooms

RECIPE LIST
BY BODY SYSTEM

SKIN

RESPIRATORY SYSTEM

IMMUNE SYSTEM

METABOLIC SYSTEM

MENTAL HEALTH & NERVOUS SYSTEM

HEART & CIRCULATION

DIGESTIVE SYSTEM

REPRODUCTIVE & URINARY SYSTEMS

INDEX

The biggest thanks of all has to go to the hundreds of people who have contacted me since the publication of *The Medicinal Chef* in 2012. Your success stories and support have moved me and motivated me to new levels. Thank you to Clare Hulton and Jenny Liddle, the two geniuses at the controls, and to all the team at Quadrille for making these books so stunning and taking my message out far and wide in the way it should be seen and heard. Tanya Murkett – thank you for inspiration and smiles every day, and also to Mum and Dad, Ramsay and Candy.

Editorial director: Anne Furniss
Creative director: Helen Lewis
Project editor: Laura Gladwin
Art direction and design: Smith & Gilmour
Photography: Martin Poole
Food stylist: Aya Nishimura
Props stylist: Polly Webb-Wilson
Production: James Finan

First published in 2014 by Quadrille Publishing Limited,
Alhambra House, 27–31 Charing Cross Road, London WC2H 0LS

www.quadrille.co.uk

Text © 2014 Dale Pinnock
Photography © 2014 Martin Poole
Design and layout © 2014 Quadrille Publishing Limited

Cataloguing in Publication Data: a catalogue record for this book
is available from the British Library.

UK Trade 978 1 84949 366 6
Export 978 1 84949 437 3

Printed in China